REFERENCE ONLY

CHILTERN CHURCHES

CHILTERN

GRAHAM MARTIN

CHURCHES

A visual survey

SPURBOOKS LIMITED

© Copyright 1972 by Graham Martin
Published by Spurbooks Limited, 88 Blind Lane, Bourne End, Bucks
Designed and produced for the publishers by Pica Editorial Limited, 26 Parkway, London NW1
ISBN 0 902875 14 0
Printed in Great Britain by Daedalus Press, Stoke Ferry, Norfolk

PREFACE

For a number of years, I, like many other people, had been wandering in and out of our parish churches all over England with only a vague appreciation of what I saw; only now has the opportunity arisen for me to make any sort of studious approach to such a vast but rewarding subject.

Since there are more than 12,500 parish churches in England, it would have been more than presumptuous to attempt a general survey, or, at the other extreme, to attempt a study of a specialized nature, for which I have not the background knowledge. Consequently I have restricted my efforts to a survey of one small part of England, the Chilterns, which embrace some seventy churches. My choice in this has been governed by several factors, not all of my own making: the Chilterns are my nearest area, given that London's suburbs are past providing interest, and that London's churches, in particular those of the City, are too profound a subject for such a first venture as this; futhermore, the natural beauty of these hills makes them a delightful area for research.

Although these churches be classified as 'poor relations', lacking all pretensions to grandeur or nobility and even most of the finer artistic points, this does not discredit them as worthy of study. For here, readily observed, is the early history of our parish churches, in many cases virtually untouched. Fortunately, for the ecclesiologist, many are as 'medieval' as any in the country; indeed, more so in certain respects, for a wealth of material has somehow survived the rabidity of the the Reformation and the vehemence of Victoriana in this Chiltern island.

Even if this were the only concern these churches would more than merit attention; as it is, there is another equally important aspect, well expressed by Baldwin Brown: 'There is a special attractiveness in the simple structure that has grown by a sort of happy accident into beauty; and it is worth while inquiring how this comes about.' I can only hope that the many photographs, my descriptions and comments, will at least indicate some solution to the inquiry, and will convey something of the incomparable charm of these churches.

Few could doubt that this is very much a visual subject, and therefore I make no apology for the exceptionally large number of illustrations which I have included; yet it is surprising that for so many years ecclesiology has been approached with such a verbal emphasis. Far too many books cry out for illustrations, and it is hardly as though subject matter were lacking. To some extent this volume has gone to the other extreme, for, while there is no lack in the quantity of photographs, there is an inadequacy in the quality of a great number which therefore fail to do justice to the subjects. This position arises largely from the fact that they have been compiled in less than a year; anyone who has tried influencing the weather to provide reasonable photographic conditions will appreciate the impossibility of the situation.

The Chiltern churches have another attraction for me in that, as far as I am aware, they have never been appreciated as a group, and they have had poor treatment individually as well. Of course, as a group they cannot compare with the more publicized ones of East Anglia or Devon, but in their own quiet, unassuming way are greatly to be admired, and one or two can stand comparison with some of our finest parish churches.

This then, is primarily a visual survey, not a text book or an authoritative work. It is also no more than an introduction to the Chilterns and their churches, so I have indicated at appropriate points the various avenues of research opened.

Finally, may I plead that the illustrations within are no substitute for reality; it is only to be hoped that they may tempt the reader to go and see for himself.

GRAHAM MARTIN

ACKNOWLEDGEMENTS

My most grateful thanks are proffered to His Grace the Duke of Bedford for permission to visit the Bedford Chapel at Chenies; to the following incumbents: Rev H. Warwick; Rev T. H. South; Rev R. Brown; Rev Kendall Baker; Rev K. Thomas; Rev J. Wildman; Rev S. W. Hagger; Rev M. Carew; Rev Trevor Jones; Rev E. J. Arnold; Rev A. Birkett; Rev S. Day; Rev Breckey; Rev D. H. Jones; Rev C. White; Rev Vickers; Rev B. W. Mackie; Rev R. E. A. Lloyd; Rev A. Speed; Rev D. Bickerton; Rev W. E. Watts; Rev Hill; Rev E. Bourne; Rev C. Plummer; Rev C. Williams; Rev Dickins; Rev E. Moreton; Rev E. J. Gargery; Rev J. James; Rev R. S. Wilkinson; Rev R. L. Parkin; Rev E. O. Williams; Rev Cavendish; Rev C. Dunford; Rev F. F. C. Roberts; Rev B. Hughes; Rev O Muspratt; Rev B. J. Corder; Rev R. Shone; Rev Hugh Jones; Rev J. S. Martin; Rev R. Arch; Rev T. McArdle; Rev E. W. Pipe; Rev A. Marple; Rev G. H. Parsons; Rev D. Bryant Bevan; Rev B. Andrewes; Rev T. K. Lowdell; Rev J. Charlesworth; Rev F. Lewis; Rev G. Milroy; Rev A. L. Evan Hopkins; and Rev S. J. Cornish.

Special thanks are also proffered to all those friends and relatives who gave encouragement or actual help, and to T. J. Lucas, and his motor-bike, without whom this project would never have been completed.

CONTENTS

TRUE NORTH

BEDFORDSHIRE

DUNSTABLE

EATON BRAY
TOTTERNHOE
EDLESBOROUGH

IVINGHOE
beacon
PITSTONE
LITTLE GADDESDEN
GRAND UNION CANAL
ALDBURY
R. GADE
GREAT GADDESDEN

TRING
NORTHCHURCH
BERKHAMSTED
HEMEL HEMPSTEAD
R. BULBOURNE

To AYLESBURY

BUCKINGHAMSHIRE

ELLESBOROUGH
UPPER
ICKNIELD WAY
WENDOVER
CHOLESBURY
ST LEONARD'S

LITTLE KIMBLE
GREAT KIMBLE
THE LEE
ABBOTS LANGLEY
KINGS LANGLEY

To THAME

MONKS RISBOROUGH
LITTLE HAMPDEN
HORSENDEN
PRINCES RISBOROUGH
GREAT HAMPDEN
BLEDLOW
SAUNDERTON
GREAT MISSENDEN
CHESHAM
FLAUNDEN

CHENNOR
CROWELL
CHESHAM BOIS

To OXFORD
RADNAGE
LITTLE MISSENDEN
CHENIES
GARRATT

LEWKNOR
AMERSHAM
BRADENHAM

ICKNIELD WAY
STOKENCHURCH
HUGHENDEN
PENN STREET

OXFORDSHIRE
WATLINGTON
WEST WYCOMBE
CHALFONT ST GILES
RICKMANSWORTH

BRITWELL
IBSTONE
HIGH WYCOMBE
R. MISBOURN

EWELME
FINGEST
PENN
CHALFONT ST PETER
R. COLNE

SWYNCOMBE
TURVILLE
PISHILL
LOUDWATER
BEACONSFIELD
To LONDON

WALLINGFORD
R. THAMES

FAWLEY
HAMBLEDEN
MARLOW
HEDGERLEY
FULMER

IPSDEN
WOBURN
BURNHAM BEECHES

MEDMENHAM
R. THAMES
STOKE POGES
UXBRIDGE

CHECKENDON
ROTHERFIELD GREYS
HENLEY
BURNHAM

ROTHERFIELD PEPPARD
BERKSHIRE
MAIDENHEAD
SLOUGH
WINDSOR

HERTS
WATFORD

Key:
A CLASS ROADS
B CLASS ROADS
LESSER ROADS
RAILWAYS
CHURCH WITH TOWER
CHURCH WITH SPIRE
CHURCH WITHOUT EITHER
COUNTY BOUNDARIES

0 1 2 3 4 5 MILES

INTRODUCTION

The Chiltern Hills form part of the chalk ridge which runs from East Anglia to Dorset, and the chalk scarp is their most distinctive feature. The very varied soil supports a variety of vegetation not found on other downland. This had particular consequences in the middle ages, because when most other downlands were being exploited for the wool trade, the Chilterns remained largely forested. Consequently the Chilterns have had no great prosperity and their churches are evidence of this.

Nor have the Chilterns a great and glorious history; even though close to the metropolis, they have remained a comparatively remote and rural area until the arrival of the twentieth century commuter. The boundaries of the Chilterns are necessarily arbitrary, except for the scarp in the west and the Thames in the south, and the map indicates the way these have been drawn.

The churches examined all belong to the Church of England, and nearly all are parish churches in their own right. Even so, at least twenty have been omitted, primarily because of lack of time; also these were all complete products, or nearly so, of the nineteenth century.

PLANS

The following are a series of available plans, mainly derived from the Victoria Counties Histories. They give a fairly comprehensive picture of the development of parish churches both in general and in particular; but there are several serious omissions like Checkendon and Swyncombe which both have apses, and Hemel Hempstead which dates from one period, 1140-1180. The scales are uniform and therefore a comparison of the respective sizes of these churches is possible, and sometimes quite startling.

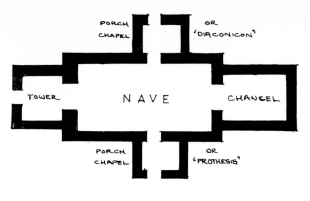

PORCH CHAPEL

OR 'DIACONICON'

NAVE

TOWER

CHANCEL

PORCH CHAPEL

OR 'PROTHESIS'

CONJECTURAL SAXON PLAN

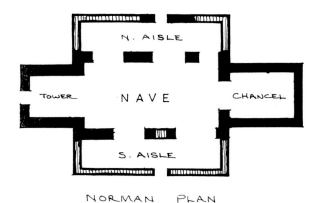

N. AISLE

TOWER

NAVE

CHANCEL

S. AISLE

NORMAN PLAN

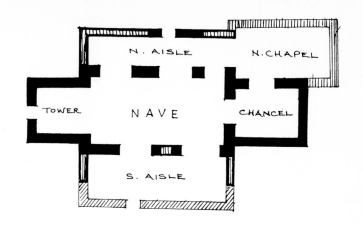

N. AISLE

N. CHAPEL

TOWER

NAVE

CHANCEL

S. AISLE

13TH & 14TH CENTURIES

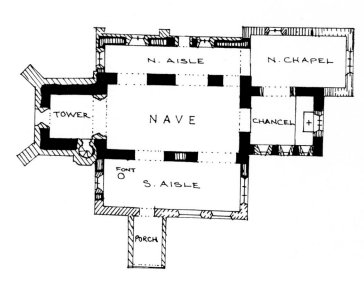

N. AISLE

N. CHAPEL

TOWER

NAVE

CHANCEL

FONT

S. AISLE

PORCH

SAXON____950-1050

NORMAN____1120-1160

____13TH CENTURY

____14TH CENTURY

____C. 1445

THE 'HOLLOW' PARTS WERE
REBUILT IN THE 17TH CENTURY.

0' 10' 20' 30' 40' 50'

SCALE IN FEET

ST JOHN
LITTLE MISSENDEN

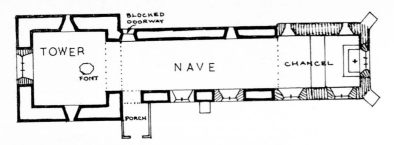

ST BARTHOLOMEW
FINGEST

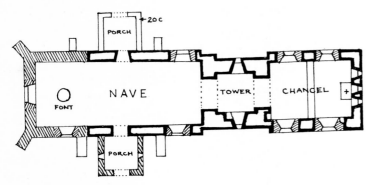

ST MARY THE VIRGIN
RADNAGE

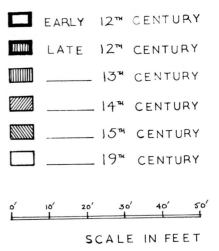

EARLY 12ᵀᴴ CENTURY

LATE 12ᵀᴴ CENTURY

_____ 13ᵀᴴ CENTURY

_____ 14ᵀᴴ CENTURY

_____ 15ᵀᴴ CENTURY

_____ 19ᵀᴴ CENTURY

SCALE IN FEET

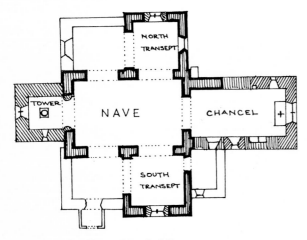

THE HOLY CROSS
SARRATT

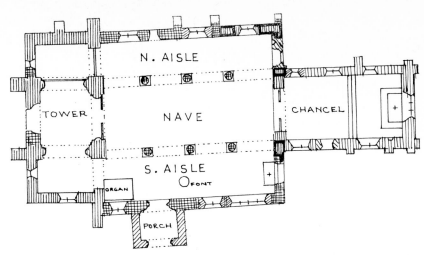

HOLY TRINITY
BLEDLOW

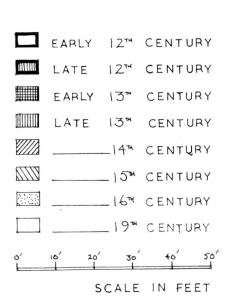

EARLY 12ᵀᴴ CENTURY

LATE 12ᵀᴴ CENTURY

EARLY 13ᵀᴴ CENTURY

LATE 13ᵀᴴ CENTURY

_____14ᵀᴴ CENTURY

_____15ᵀᴴ CENTURY

_____16ᵀᴴ CENTURY

_____19ᵀᴴ CENTURY

0'   10'   20'   30'   40'   50'

SCALE IN FEET

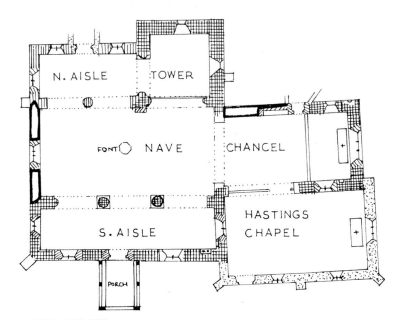

ST GILES
STOKE POGES

ST PETER'S
BERKHAMSTEAD

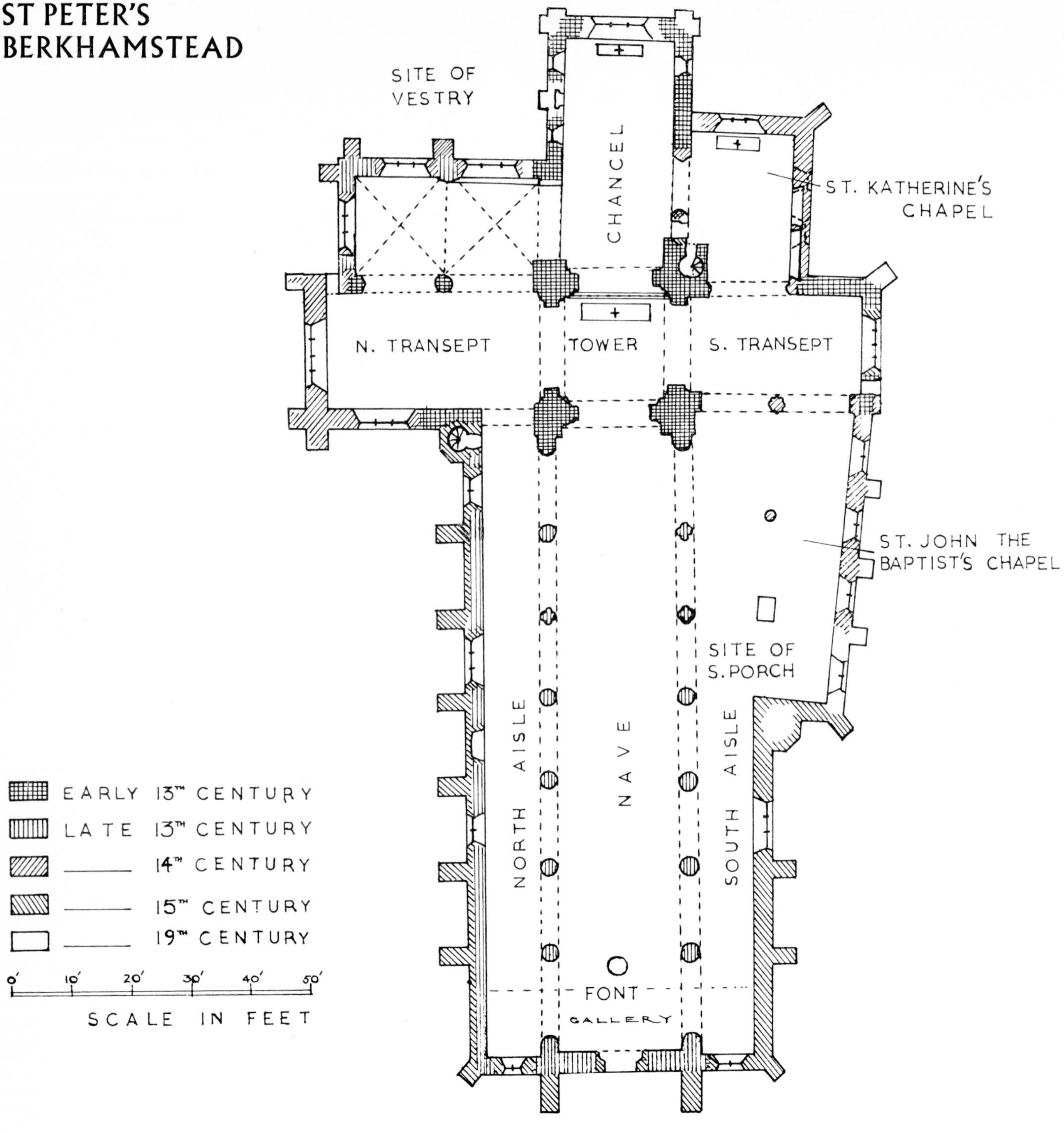

SITE OF
VESTRY

ST. KATHERINE'S
CHAPEL

CHANCEL

N. TRANSEPT   TOWER   S. TRANSEPT

ST. JOHN THE
BAPTIST'S CHAPEL

SITE OF
S. PORCH

NORTH AISLE   NAVE   SOUTH AISLE

FONT
GALLERY

EARLY 13ᵀᴴ CENTURY

LATE 13ᵀᴴ CENTURY

_____ 14ᵀᴴ CENTURY

_____ 15ᵀᴴ CENTURY

_____ 19ᵀᴴ CENTURY

0'   10'   20'   30'   40'   50'

SCALE IN FEET

14

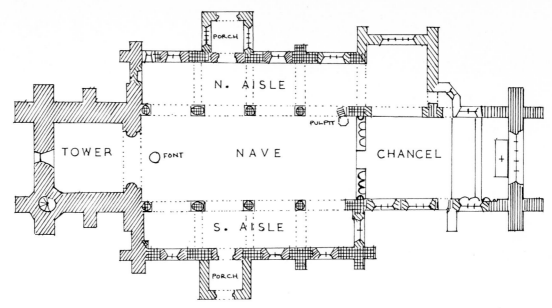

ST MARY
EDLESBOROUGH

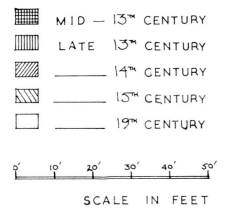

MID — 13ᵀᴴ CENTURY

LATE 13ᵀᴴ CENTURY

_____ 14ᵀᴴ CENTURY

_____ 15ᵀᴴ CENTURY

_____ 19ᵀᴴ CENTURY

0'   10'   20'   30'   40'   50'

SCALE IN FEET

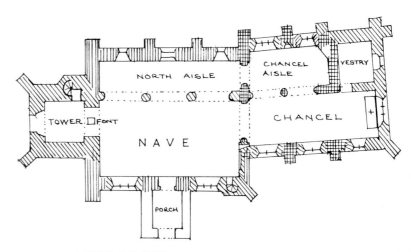

ST MARY
PITSTONE

15

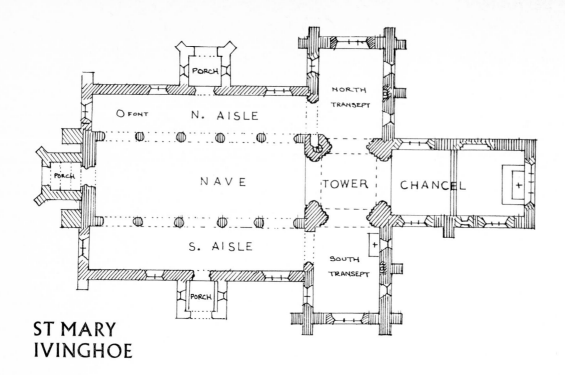

**ST MARY
IVINGHOE**

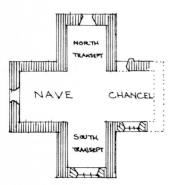

**OLD CHURCH
FLAUNDEN**

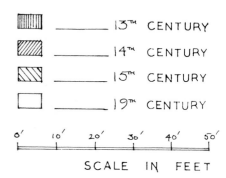

	_____	13TH CENTURY
	_____	14TH CENTURY
	_____	15TH CENTURY
	_____	19TH CENTURY

0'   10'   20'   30'   40'   50'

SCALE IN FEET

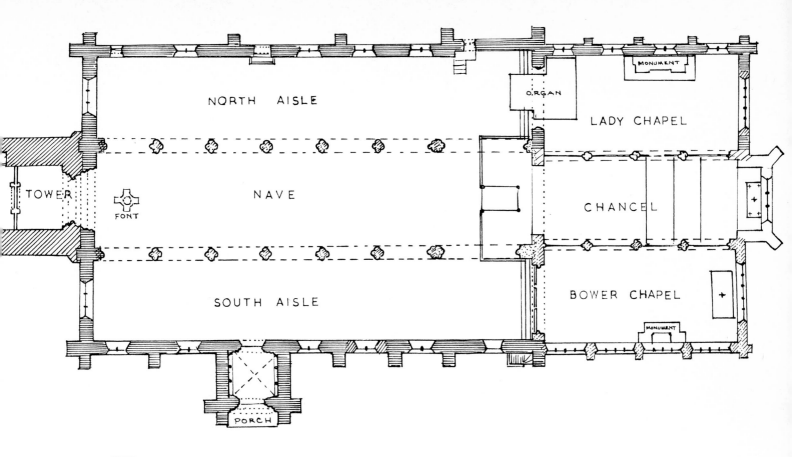

NORTH AISLE

TOWER

NAVE

FONT

SOUTH AISLE

PORCH

ORGAN

MONUMENT

LADY CHAPEL

CHANCEL

BOWER CHAPEL

MONUMENT

|||||| LATE 13ᵀᴴ CENTURY

EARLY 15ᵀᴴ CENTURY

_____ C. 1490

_____ C. 1500

_____ 1508-9

_____ 19ᵀᴴ CENTURY

0' 10' 20' 30' 40' 50'

SCALE IN FEET

THE HIGH ALTAR IS NOW
SEVERAL FEET FORWARD OF
THE POSITION INDICATED HERE
THERE WAS ORIGINALLY A
CENTRAL TOWER TILL 1508

**ALL SAINTS
HIGH WYCOMBE**

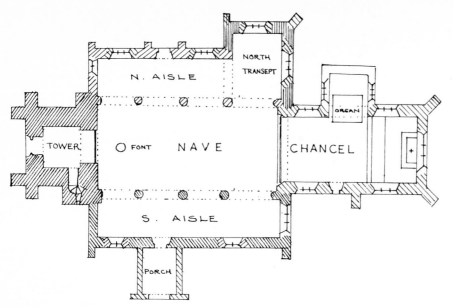

ST DUNSTAN
MONKS RISBOROUGH

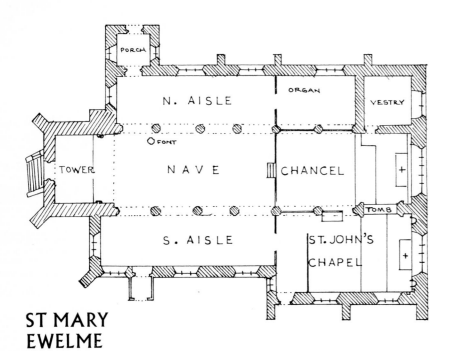

ST MARY
EWELME

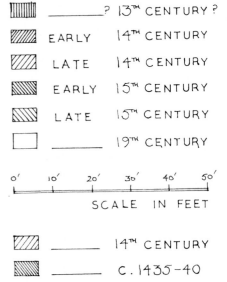

? 13TH CENTURY ?
EARLY 14TH CENTURY
LATE 14TH CENTURY
EARLY 15TH CENTURY
LATE 15TH CENTURY
19TH CENTURY

0'   10'   20'   30'   40'   50'

SCALE IN FEET

14TH CENTURY
C. 1435-40

EXTERIORS AND INTERIORS

Many of the Chiltern churches are represented here and interesting comparisons can be drawn; for instance, the similarities between Chinnor and Bledlow churches. Features that are common to the Chiltern churches may also be ascertained, although one can go little further than determining that flint work is universal. However, some of the towers seem to have common characteristics, and this might be worth examining further.

The churches have been loosely arranged, often arbitrarily, according to the style or period to which the church as a whole is most closely connected. Thus a medieval church which had been largely rebuilt by the Victorians, such as Beaconsfield, would be classed as nineteenth century. Whereas the Perpendicular was the most prosperous for the East Anglian churches, the predominance of the Decorated style would suggest that this was the most prosperous era in the Chiltern churches' history.

Both interiors and exteriors are marked by a common simplicity that is broken by touches of richness and colour that are often unexpected.

NORMAN

THE LEE

RADNAGE

FINGEST

EARLY ENGLISH

IVINGHOE

BLEDLOW

DECORATED

ALDBURY

CHINNOR

GREAT
MISSENDEN

25

PERPENDICULAR

PRINCES
RISBOROUGH

BRADENHAM

CHENIES

ST LEONARDS

MEDMENHAM

STONEWORK

Abbots Langley
late Norman

Bledlow
thirteenth century

There are many interesting decorative details to be found such as arches, arcades and capitals: twelfth century arcading at Abbots Langley and Hemel Hempstead, where there are also carved chancel arch capitals resembling those at Checkendon; stiff-leafed capitals and arcading of the thirteenth century at Bledlow, Ivinghoe, Pitstone, Eaton Bray, Flamstead, and Great Gaddesden; and slender fifteenth century arcading, with carved beasts, at Tring.

Other details to be found include blank arcading at Burnham; window arcading at Princes Risborough; and many corbels and carved fragments, often out of context, as at Little Hampden and Aldbury.

Checkendon
Norman chancel arch detail

Tring
fifteenth century arcade detail

Hemel Hempstead
Norman

DOORS, DOORWAYS AND PORCHES

In the Saxon period there were normally two doorways to the church, in the north and south walls of the nave; invariably each had a porch. The conjectural plan of Little Missenden church illustrates this point. But the Normans, for some obscure reason, had little use for the porch. Their doorways, often highly ornamented, were left quite open to the elements; the desirability of the porch in the English climate was, however, rapidly appreciated. Thereafter the porch grew in size and importance. It was often the seat of local government, and much business, both public and private, was conducted there. Reminders of those days are the public notices which are still pinned to the noticeboards or on the doors. Nor was the porch purely a temporal place; many services began there, for instance the ceremonies of marriage and baptism. Not all porches were as widely used, many were not large enough; but many were built expressly for such purposes. In the fourteenth century these sometimes included an upper story, which became commonplace in the fifteenth century. Such an upper chamber may have been used as an occasional chapel, by a guild, or by nightwatchmen, or as a store or library after the Reformation. Where they were big enough, schools were conducted there, usually by a priest. Sometimes when there was an upper storey the porch would be vaulted, as at Chesham, or even at Chinnor where there is only a porch. In the fifteenth century the porch reached the culmination of its development, being large,

Little Hampden

generally two-storied, shafted and pinnacled, image-ridden and embattled. West porches also occur, but are rare. The west front of the English parish church has never been of great importance, as on the Continent, mainly because of the characteristic English west tower. Many churches, in fact, have no west door at all. Apart from west porches formed by the lower storey of the tower, about the only true west porch is the fine fifteenth century vaulted one at Ivinghoe. There are a number of large porches in the Chilterns, as at Great Hampden, and elsewhere.

Little Hampden church is endowed with a very unusual porch for the area. Here the main entrance is on the north, and the porch is tall, two-storied and half-timbered, dating from the Elizabethan period. The upper storey is used as the bell-cote. Otherwise nearly all the Chiltern churches have ancient porches though many are of little interest.

Looking further into the porch, at the doorways, it is often surprising to find a wealth of lovely

Bradenham

Checkendon

stonework detail. The south doorway at Bradenham may well be Saxon; a church did exist before the Conquest, and the detail looks correct though it has been cited by some people as Norman. Checkendon church definitely has a Norman south doorway, and the whole church is of the period complete with an apse, a rarity, and some good stonework detail. Rather later, and more refined, dating from about 1150, is the fine work at the imposing and complete Norman church at Hemel Hempstead. Here there is a good west doorway. The Normans seem to have been responsible for the introduction of the west door.

Of later doorways, there is a very elaborately moulded fourteenth century south doorway at Wendover, and good early fifteenth century examples at Monks Risborough. There is a fifteenth century west doorway to Amersham church. Countless other doorways are of medieval origin.

Bledlow
note the stoup

Finally to the doors themselves; again, a large number of doors are two or three hundred years old, and quite a number are medieval. That at Fulmer, taken from the old church, is hung on strap hinges and is very heavily studded with nails. The south door at Monks Risborough dates from the early fifteenth century like the doorway itself; it still has its original hinges, and is ornamented with a decorated lock and latch, and many rose-headed nails. But the most remarkable door of all is at Eaton Bray, where the south door is completely covered with beautiful coiled iron-work; this was executed by Thomas of Leighton (of nearby Leighton Buzzard) in the thirteenth century. He was also responsible for the superb Eleanor Grille in Westminster Abbey. There are other medieval doors at Bledlow, Ivinghoe and in many other churches, and a sixteenth century door to the Hastings Chapel at Stoke Poges.

SEDILIA

Sedilia is only the Latin plural for seats; these are, or were, for the priests during parts of a service. In the middle ages stone seats were built into the wall of the chancel, always on the south side, or near side altars. Although a sedile, a single seat, occurs frequently, as do triple sedilia, double ones are very rare. This is because a priest would either officiate alone, as in many of the smaller churches, or helped by a deacon and sub-deacon. When there were three they would occupy the seats in order of precedence from the east.

Hambleden

Chinnor

Sometimes, to mark this grading, the seats were arranged on different levels.

At Hambleden is a fine triple sedilia of the Decorated period, very well restored; and an even finer and more elaborate group at Lewknor, quite unexpected in such an unprepossessing church. There is another triple group at Chinnor with simple mouldings. All these are well restored and in use.

Wooden sedilia appear to have been very rare but there are two fifteenth century oak sedilia in Chesham Bois church.

After the Reformation, when many were damaged or even destroyed, they were generally not used, but in the nineteenth century a large number were restored and employed again. Restoration depended on the incumbent; in a number of cases sedilia were completely removed.

New sedilia are rare, but can be found, as at Chesham where there is a very pleasing group, carved in unstained oak.

Other sedilia, nearly all single and very simple, may be found at Aldbury, Burnham, Edlesborough, The Lee, Medmenham (dating from 1906), Great Missenden, Princes Risborough (a sedile in the south aisle), St Leonards and Sarratt. The last is a sedile made by cutting down one half of a double piscina. Quite often window sills were cut down to form them as well.

PISCINAE

Stoke Poges

A piscina is a drain, leading to consecrated soil, where the washing of the vessels and the priests' hands is carried out. In the middle ages these were of stone and recessed in the south wall of the chancel, or in aisle or transept walls when there were side altars. When there were sedilia as well, the piscina was often incorporated in the group as at Hambleden, Chinnor, Lewknor, and Princes Risborough.

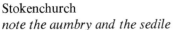

Stokenchurch
note the aumbry and the sedile

In the reign of Edward I, double piscinae were ordered: separate bowls for the washing of the vessels, and the priests' hands. This order, however, seems to have been widely disregarded, for double piscinae remain comparatively rare. Examples may be found at Stoke Poges, Chalfont St Giles and elsewhere.

Because of side altars, so numerous in the middle ages, many churches today still have more than one piscina; both Berkhamsted and Kings Langley churches have three.

A vast number of piscinae survive from the thirteenth century onwards, all medieval, and nearly every church in the Chilterns has at least one.

STOUPS

Stoups are stone containers for holy water, attached to a wall, and are generally to be found in porches or close to main entrances. They are all medieval in origin and most were damaged or destroyed at the Reformation. Some may still be found at Bledlow, (see 'Doorways'), Chalfont St Giles, Chesham, Ellesborough, Great Hampden, Great Missenden, Monks Risborough and High Wycombe.

SQUINTS

A squint, or hagioscope, is a hole cut through a wall or pier to give a view of the high altar from an otherwise viewless position, as in many aisles. Contrary to the general idea, these squints were not intended for all the people in the aisles. One has only to try looking through from various positions to realise this is impossible. It is now thought that the squint was only for the use of the priest officiating at side altars, and the purpose was to enable him to synchronize his celebration of the mass with that at the high altar. Squints may be seen at Aldbury, Chalfont St Giles, Great Hampden, Horsenden, Pitstone and Stokenchurch.

NICHES AND IMAGE BRACKETS

Ewelme

Both these features were as prolific before the Reformation as the images they held; most were destroyed or badly mutilated with the hated images.

Niches may be found at Amersham, Bledlow, Edlesborough and Great Hampden; copies of the original ones at Hughenden and Great Missenden and very mutilated examples at Monks Risborough and at Ewelme. The two niches at the latter church are both fifteenth century and have been restored complete with their original colouring (see 'Wall paintings').

There are brackets at Monks Risborough and Ewelme.

The majority of niches and brackets surviving are from the fifteenth century, when the fashion for images was at its height.

38

EASTER SEPULCHRES

In the middle ages, on Good Friday, the blessed sacrament was placed in some recess until the morning of Easter Day to symbolize Christ in the burial chamber and his subsequent resurrection. To provide for this, a recess was made always in the north wall of the chancel; very few exist, however, and it would appear that most Easter sepulchres must have been less permanent, of wood. Where they do exist as a recess there is often doubt as to their authenticity, as at Sarratt and Stoke Poges. This is partly because tomb recesses were sometimes requisitioned for the purpose. In the Chilterns only those at Ivinghoe and Stokenchurch seem authentic.

AUMBRIES

Aumbries and Easter sepulchres are sometimes confused also because both could be simple, undecorated wall recesses. An aumbry is a locker, either of wood, or stone set in the wall, used to store the vessels. These may occur in, or on, either the north or south walls, and this adds to the confusion. In the Chilterns all are plain wall recesses which would once have had wooden doors to them – Swyncombe still has. Others may be seen at Bledlow, Chalfont St Giles, Pitstone, Sarratt, Stokenchurch, Wooburn and elsewhere.

FONTS

The font, which is basically nothing more than a vessel to contain water for baptism, arises out of the Christian ritual of purifying the convert and initiating him into the 'body' of Christ; this relies upon the Scriptures for its authority, and the early Church in this country appears to have immersed rather than sprinkled the candidates. The size of pre-Reformation fonts bear this out; certainly most of the early ones were big enough to immerse a baby, but as the middle ages waned, fonts tended to decrease in their water capacity. One must suspect that sprinkling was practised equally with immersion. Certainly sprinkling would have been imperative for adult converts, and particularly in the Saxon period it would have been a practical necessity arising out of the problem of baptizing converts by the hundred. There is still doubt as to whether or not one or other of these ceremonies was in fact performed by the Christian church at its inception; such a doubt was expressed as long ago as the seventeenth century with the foundation of the Anabaptist sect, who believe in total immersion, and baptism of adults only. Certainly after the Reformation the established church practised only sprinkling, witness the small size of new fonts. The return to larger fonts in the Victorian era was a sop to the 'Gothick' taste rather than a change in dogma. It is interesting that the Book of Common Prayer still recommends immersion.

Of fonts before the Norman invasion, little is known; probably very few exist, and the authenticity of some of these is open to doubt. It is important to remember that the Saxon and Norman styles were by no means alien to each other, since both belong to the Romanesque group. The difficulty is to distinguish Norman fonts from Saxon; these distinctions depend on subtlety of shape and the character of the decoration.

No Chiltern church possesses a Saxon font, except for the extremely dubious 'egg cup' at Radnage, probably because there were few permanent stone churches in the area before the Conquest. Even where such a church existed, as at Little Missenden, the Normans supplied a font to replace any predecessor there might have been.

There are, however, many Norman fonts and these probably survived because the Chilterns, in later years, were never very wealthy, thus any building developments were retarded. The very simplest, and the earliest, was the tub, or cylinder; these may be dated about 1100 when decoration was still in abatement. Examples of these occur at Ibstone, Little Kimble, The Lee, and Turville, ranging in date from *c* 1100-1200, if it is at all possible to date them apart. They are all, one will notice, in small and generally remote churches, and this may partially account for their survival.

An interesting Norman diversion from the stone font was the lead font, of which only a dozen or so have survived, though doubtless they were almost as rare in their time; the Chiltern churches may, or may not, have an example at Penn. Unfortunately the bowl shape belongs to the transitional period, about 1200; even then there is doubt, for it has been suggested that the bowl is seventeenth century, and merely lead-covered, a theory worth testing. It would be very unusual if it were so, and the Purbeck marble stem with base and circular plinth are certainly about 1200. If it is genuine, it is unique.

From the early tub shape there developed rather larger cylinders, decorated all over with a low relief pattern. In the Chilterns there are two of these, at Lewknor and Hambleden. Both are very large and almost perfect cylinders, more upright, one will note, than the earlier fonts. The Hambleden font is the finest of the early Norman period

Little Kimble

Lewknor

in the Chilterns, being carved with a low relief pattern; the side is ornamented with large diamond shapes, each containing a floreated cross, and the spandrels are filled with single arms of such crosses. The top edge has an indented moulding. As with nearly all fonts, the interior is lead-lined and there are remains of the clamps which once held the lid. This font may well date from the early twelfth century and is certainly prior to 1190, which generally marks the end of the Norman period and the start of the Early English. The Lewknor font, with its circular repeating motifs, is more interesting because it sets a problem. On comparing the two, one's immediate reaction is to the disparity between the decoration. It is just possible that this font is unusually early, and might have been executed by a Saxon craftsman. The Hambleden font, and the other early ones, all reveal a hardness of line, an angularity, compatible with a time of conquest and evidenced in contemporary decoration; towards the end of the twelfth century the lines and shapes became softer, to form the Transitional type.

Although the tub or cylindrical shape is typical of the Norman period there was some experiment and development in the overall shape; such a one is in Rotherfield Greys church. This is nearly a cube and dates from about the mid twelfth century; it is unique in the Chilterns, and rare even further afield, but as an experiment it does not appear to have had any successors.

Fonts that were part of a successive development are those at Rotherfield Peppard, with its cable-roll, and the very simple bowl and stem at Swyn-combe. Both date from about 1190. Continuing this development, probably the most distinctive of all products of the Chilterns is the group of fonts known as 'Aylesbury' after the font in that church; these fonts belong primarily to the Transitional period, *c* 1200, but they cover a number of years, apparently from about 1190 to about 1210. Evidently they are the work of a school of masons, if not one mason, and may be products of the Totternhoe quarries in the very north of the Chilterns. These quarries have had a great influence on the hills for they provided the only good stone, and even then it weathered poorly. This influence has largely been confined to the northern half because the southern Chilterns would have obtained most of their stone from Oxfordshire.

Also, being situated at the northern tip of the Chilterns, the Totternhoe quarries' influence extended well into Bedfordshire, and, indeed, a number of similar fonts are said to exist there. Therefore the 'Aylesbury' group ought not, perhaps, to be classed as a Chiltern product, yet the majority of these fonts are to be found within its bounds or very close by. They are to be found at Aylesbury in the vale, Bledlow, Buckland, in the vale but close to Tring, Chenies, Great Kimble, Great Missenden, Little Missenden, Pitstone, Monks Risborough, Saunderton, Wing, not far from Totternhoe and at Weston Turville, also in the vale but not far from Wendover. Note that they all occur in, or close to, the northern half of the hills. They all have in common most of the

Swyncombe

following characteristics: a circular bowl, fluted for the most part, with a band of enrichment around the top; a cable-roll connecting the bowl and the base, and a square base but formed like an inverted cushion cap with foliage decoration in double or single lunettes on each face. In further detail, the Bledlow font has a very short stem between cable-roll and base, and double lunettes.

43

Chenies

bowl is rather different from that on others. Pitstone font conforms to the description, but that at Monks Risborough has a circular base instead of the usual type. The last is at Saunderton which also lacks the square base, and has different decoration at the top of the bowl. Altogether they are a remarkable group, almost certainly unique in England, and reveal their development in a most instructive way.

It is only a short step to the font at Great Hampden; this is a real outcome of the main group, bearing most of their characteristics but with a change in the detail and much greater refinement. This places the font at the end of the Transitional period, sometime in the early thirteenth century, and predicting the Early English style.

Great Hampden

That at Chenies also has a short stem, but without a true cable-roll, single lunettes, and very well defined enrichment around the top of the bowl. Great Kimble font has double lunettes, and is probably the largest of them all and particularly fine, occupying a commanding position in the centre of the nave. That at Great Missenden has the usual base with single lunettes and all the other features, but the bowl has been recut, or replaced, probably in the fifteenth century.

It is interesting that a church very close by, Little Missenden, should also have one of these fonts; this has single lunettes and all the other features except that the enrichment around the top of the

44

During the Transitional and Early English periods there was another development of the font known, appropriately enough, as the 'table top'. The early beginings of this are very well illustrated by the font at Chalfont St Giles, which dates from about 1200; note the square shallow top supported by five shafts which were restored in 1861. It has been suggested that the faces of the bowl were originally arcaded. This font should be compared with that at Eaton Bray and the tremendous change noted. The latter, in marble, is well moulded and carved, and dates from the mid thirteenth century. There was another at Sarratt, which was replaced by a copy in the nineteenth century. But this type appears to have lost favour and to have been discontinued in later years.

The font at Hughenden dates from the early thirteenth century and is Early English in detail; however, the cylindrical shape is a remarkable throwback to the Norman period, and therefore would appear to be out of line with the general development of fonts.

Stokenchurch font was, it is said, also originally early thirteenth century but was recut in the fifteenth century. Certainly the present simple angular mouldings suggest a fifteenth century date. Similarly, the bowl of Hedgerley font is claimed to be twelfth century but recut in the fifteenth century when the eight small carvings were made; also a new stem and base were fitted.

After the thirteenth century, any detailed development is almost impossible to trace, particularly

Chalfont St Giles

among the Chiltern fonts. Indeed, of all the other medieval fonts only one, apparently, is fourteenth century, that at Ellesborough. The octagonal bowl has an ogee profile and flowing tracery; the base and stem are modern but presumably copies of the originals.

Of the fifteenth century there are many fonts, few distinguished, and all varied but with certain common characteristics: these include an octagonal vertically sided bowl on an octagonal stem with a similarly shaped base. The simplest of this

45

Hughenden

and most elaborate, is that at Ewelme; here the quatrefoiled faces also enclose shields whilst the stem is elaborately panelled and traceried. The font cover is superb. This font, like the rest of the church, is strongly reminiscent of the East Anglian style, due to the then patron, the Duke of Suffolk.

After the Reformation, few new fonts were necessary because the old ones were acceptable to the reformed church. Only in the case of new churches, a rarity then, were new fonts made, and such a case was Fulmer. This church, built in 1610, is claimed to be the second to be built after the Reformation; the font dates from its founding. It is very unusual, a rarity, and less than twelve such fonts exist. The body and stem is of panelled wood and inset in the top is a small stone bowl; this is a direct confirmation of sprinkling as the practise for baptism by the established church. Up to the restorations of 1877-84, this font was in use but was then discarded in favour of the present one. The Jacobean font was lovingly restored by Clive Rouse in 1959.

All the other fonts made before the nineteenth century also confirm sprinkling by the size of their bowls; thus the fonts at Chesham Bois, and Little Hampden. That at West Wycombe, however, is completely remarkable and the only other wooden font in the Chilterns. The tripod stand has a serpent entwined around it, and the minute basin actually has birds standing on it! These, surely, are true eighteenth century conceits.

type are the plain sided ones at Northchurch and Checkendon, one at Edlesborough with simple quatrefoils on each face, a similar one at Flaunden and an unusual one at Fingest. This has a rather taller bowl than most, the panels have trefoil heads, and the stem is recent; it might well prove to be of the late fourteenth century.

A little more elaborate is Abbots Langley font which has faces with quatrefoils enclosing shields and evangelical symbols alternately. The best,

Almost all the other Chiltern churches not yet mentioned have Victorian fonts; this is because at so many nineteenth century restorations the older fonts were often discarded for new ones, not that these would perform their task any better but because of a great parochial pride, a belief that in the new fonts they were continuing the medieval tradition, and an inexplicable adoration of one particular style as the perfect medieval form. The results, if not copies, are startling and often in very bad taste.

Even though later medieval fonts are not very well represented in the Chiltern churches, as they are in the East Anglian churches, the collection of early material is truly remarkable.

Beaconsfield

Fulmer

FONT COVERS

All fonts were covered in the middle ages; they were locked down as well because the holy water was only changed at Easter and Whitsun, and there was the danger that the water might be stolen by witches. The medieval cover took the form either of a triptych cupboard or a simple lift-off type; the latter was far commoner. None are known earlier than the fourteenth century but from hasps and staples still left on fonts they must have been in use before then.

In the Chilterns there is only one from before the Reformation, at Ewelme. This is a superb fifteenth century spire, with four stages of tracery, over ten feet high, and similar to, but slightly smaller than, the famous one at Ufford in Suffolk. The cover at Little Kimble looks medieval but may be nineteenth century, though it is rather elaborate for that era.

Many covers were destroyed at the Reformation but, later, Archbishop Laud, during the reign of Charles I, ordered covers to be fitted and the seventeenth century covers surviving must date from about then. There are examples of these at Chalfont St Giles, Edlesborough, Hedgerley and Stokenchurch. All the other font covers date from the nineteenth century, and few are worthy of note.

Hedgerley

48

ALTARS
AND
REREDOSES

Little Hampden

In the middle ages altars were of stone; at the Reformation they were all broken, cut up or just thrown out into the churchyard. Tables were then used, and have continued so with few exceptions. Occasionally the stone slabs have been rediscovered and restored. That at Little Hampden was put back in 1948 where it forms a very delightful and simple altar. Many Jacobean altar tables may be found, as at Eaton Bray, though they are generally hidden by the frontals. And, of course, there are many later altar tables, most of a plain type.

Behind the medieval altar one would always have found a reredos. This may have been of wood, stone or three alabaster panels forming a triptych, but the carvings they bore were basically common to all. There was a central crucifixion, other scenes from the life of Christ, and

49

Rotherfield Peppard

sometimes lives of the saints. These were particular targets of the reformers and none survives complete in the Chilterns. At Pitstone there is a fragment of a fifteenth century stone reredos; and at Hambleden is a beautiful fifteenth century Nottingham alabaster of the nativity which once probably formed part of a triptych.

During the sixteenth and seventeenth centuries reredoses of any form were rarely used; towards the end of the seventeenth century, however, decorative panelling was employed behind the altar, and this developed in the eighteenth century. At Rotherfield Peppard is a remarkable and very fine eighteenth century reredos of French origin. This is covered by a copy of Leonardo da Vinci's 'Last Supper', executed in marquetry.

Not surprisingly, the nineteenth century religious revival brought an outburst of reredoses in stone, marble, and wood, carved, gilded and highly coloured. For the most part they are dreadful, including that at Little Gaddesden. On the saving side are a very fine series of reredoses, dating from about the turn of the century, by Ninian Comper. One of these may be seen at Ellesborough. Equally fine are those at Tring and High Wycombe.

50

IN MEMORIAM

Certainly since Christianity reached our shores the Christian church has always buried its dead; cremation is a comparatively modern development in this country and, to the medieval mind, would have been far too akin to the flames of hell to find favour. The burial of the complete body was, of course, imperative if the literal resurrection of the body was to come. One must suspect, however, that by the fifteenth century some people were becoming sceptical, and cynical, about the Last Judgment, an impending doom so vividly portrayed in contemporary paintings which was always foretold but never came nearer.

The early Christians here were buried simply, with little or no marking, and even the greater folk have left no memorials, though these would certainly have perished in the course of time. The common people were buried without any indication as to who they were, and this continued into the eighteenth century, and, for the poorest, even to this very day. Coffins too were only for the wealthy before the seventeenth century, and uncoffined burials were still taking place last century. The coffin was really only a method of keeping the body together a little longer for the great resurrection of the dead. On the other hand, once the marks of an ordinary burial had disappeared, new graves were dug and disturbed bones were placed in the local charnel house, a practice which would shock most people today. The result of continuous burials can be seen nowadays in the old churchyards where both paths and church are well below the grave level, as at Bledlow or Northchurch.

Despite the wealthy medieval man's concern for his body, it was merely an extra safeguard compared with the general fear for the soul; the passing bell, for example, a custom not peculiar to Christianity, was intended to protect the soul from demons while on its way to purgatory or hell. But it is the chantries which give us the best idea of this awful dread which the medieval Christian suffered for his soul. These chantries were at first established by the wealthy – wealth could do wonders in matters of religion then – and a priest was appointed in perpetuity to intercede for the souls of the deceased, and of other members of the family as they died. Guilds and other brotherly associations followed by establishing their own chantries; they did not always leave the matter to the priest alone but went as a body and prayed for their deceased members. These chantry priests were quite separate from the regular parish priest and his subordinates in whose church these chantries were generally founded. Altogether, little expense was spared when so much was at stake.

Perhaps it was the greatest evil of the medieval church, next to idolatry, that it was believed that God could be appeased, or bought off, by vast gifts to the church, that sins could be excused by the purchase of indulgences, that, in effect, worldly possessions could be exchanged for salvation in the next world. What the church gained in beauty and richness of appointments, it certainly lost in spiritual values.

Whereas the soul was the problem before the Reformation, after, the body gradually took the ascendency. The result, at first, was a new breath of piety. Then followed a loss of humility, and increasing ostentation leading to the self-glorification of the eighteenth century, the ghastly sentiment of the nineteenth century, and the bewilderment of the present. This glorification of the body, combined with the evolution of democracy, has led from a situation where only the local demagogue had a monument, and the poor were but a heap of bones and a mound of earth, to where the inviolable grave of every freeman sprouts marble in civic fields, while many churches stand forlorn amidst their closed yards of mouldering sentiment.

Kings Langley

The earliest memorials appear to be simple slabs, rarely with any inscription, but with just a decorative cross or so. Examples of these may be seen at Sarratt, at Tring, where the slab bears a cross and two hinge-like scrolls, and may be late twelfth century, and at Stoke Poges, of about the same date, which is remarkable because of the inscription, in Norman-French: 'All those who pass by here Pray for the soul of this one; William of Wytermerse he had for name; God to him grant true pardon. So be it.' This is particularly unusual because names rarely appear before 1400: coats-of-arms were more than sufficient for an illiterate populace. These arms were at first painted and so have now disappeared. These monuments would all have been within the church for there were no churchyard monuments before the Reformation; the churchyard was not just a burial ground but a clear space which functioned much as did the later village greens – they were used for pageants and processions, fairs, markets, church sales, and much secular business generally. The distinction between spiritual and temporal, church and state, was barely distinguishable at first, the two being completely interwoven. In the late medieval period a gulf began to appear, and the Reformation, although it set up the established church under state control, actually brought about the real separation of the two.

From the slabs grew the tomb chests, really coffins raised above ground; the Chiltern churches possess several, some very fine indeed. The oldest by far, and quite the finest, is the Langley tomb at Kings Langley; this was erected to Edmund of Langley, fifth son of Edward III, and founder of the White Rose faction. It was originally in the church of the Dominican friars which existed not far away till the Dissolution, and was brought here in 1575. The top slab was cut from a huge altar stone some ten feet long, now seven feet by three feet, as is shown by the three consecration crosses which remain out of five. This top may date only from the tomb's move here because the tomb of so important a person must surely have borne an effigy on top; this was probably destroyed at the time of the Reformation just as the heraldic carving on the east side was badly damaged. The remaining carving of shields is very fine and has been splendidly repainted. The original tomb dates from between 1393 and 1398.

That at Aldbury is a very late example, a 'London' type executed in Purbeck marble, and has brasses inlaid in the top to Sir Ralph Varney, who died in 1546, and his family. Of the same type, and similar date, is that in Chalfont St Giles church. At Chesham Bois is a tomb chest of 1585 (after the Reformation), which has an inscription and the arms and crest of Sir John Cheyne above it. And in Berkhampsted church is a particularly late example to John Sayer, head cook to Charles II, who died in 1682. These tomb chests are but one facet of the vast memorial ensemble of our parish churches; in the middle ages a number bore effigies, those hopefully pious images of the often impious rich. These effigies include the finest surviving examples of medieval English figure sculpture since most went undamaged at the Reformation. It is very important to remember that likeness was not the goal of either sculptor or patron, but a form of ideal, an abstraction; it might even be described as a form of symbolism, which itself pervades all medieval art. Other than the face and the pose, however, every other detail may be taken as correct, thus providing invaluable sources of information.

One of the most interesting facts relates to the pose; this proves extremely revealing as to the attitude of an age, from the thirteenth century, when effigies first appear, to the virtual end of memorial figure-sculpture in the nineteenth century. Throughout the middle ages, effigies remained recumbent and in an attitude of piety, but the detail changed from a simple abstraction to realism. This is indicative of the increasing wealth, particularly in the fifteenth century, and a rising materialistic outlook. The earliest effigy in the Chilterns is that in Ivinghoe church; this is of a priest in mass vestments with the head and feet defaced, and lies in a later recess. The effigy most probably represents Peter Chacepore, who was rector from 1241-1254.

Almost as old is that in the North chapel at Hughenden; this depicts a knight with legs crossed, and dates from about 1285. It has been altered in some of its details, however, in the sixteenth century. In fact this is one of a most odd collection of effigies in this church; there are six in all, and were assembled by the Wellesbourne family in the sixteenth century. Any that were old were altered, and at least three are copies or mock-ups of earlier work, all this to prove their connection with the De Montfort family! There is a knight in chain and plate armour of the early fourteenth century in which the forearms have been broken off and crudely recarved in the body. These effigies of the fourteenth century may be distinguished from the earlier ones by the more realistic and finer carving, some relaxation in the pose, and in the general use of tomb recesses, often with elaborately moulded heads. Then there are three effigies of knights in plate armour

Hughenden

carved in low relief; these are sixteenth century. Almost certainly of the same date is the sixth effigy, a strange figure depicting a corpse lying on a shroud; in a cavity in the breast a small figure with outstretched arms symbolizes the departing spirit. Despite the copying and alteration, the details, apart from the heraldry, may be taken as accurate. These effigies are therefore of importance.

55

Chenies

At Chenies, in the Bedford Chapel, are effigies
to Sir John Cheyne, the Lollard, and his wife,
dating from about 1400; the man is unfinished
from the waist down.

Probably a little earlier is the monument in Berkhamsted church; here, there are effigies apparently of a member of the Incent family and his wife,
but both are badly damaged.

Berkhamstead

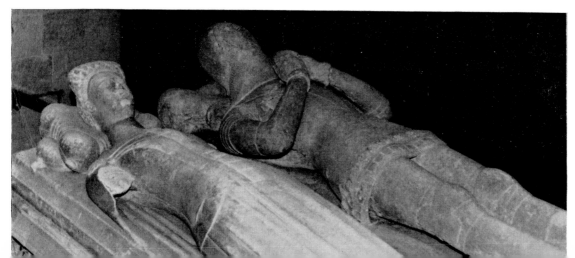

Ewelme

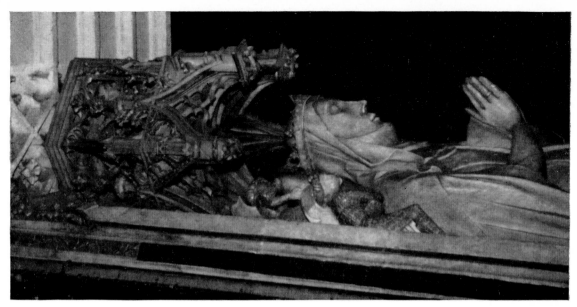

In the fifteenth century the zenith of this recumbent effigy form was reached; they are indeed the finest in craftsmanship, but these effigies always bear a realism that contrasts strangely not only with that of the thirteenth century but with the whole conception of the importance of the soul in medieval thought. Even so, there is no doubt that these late effigies present a magnificent appearance, albeit a worldly one.

A very fine example is that in Aldbury church to Sir Robert Whittingham and his wife; he died in 1471. The figures lie on a free standing tomb chest, which is panelled on the sides with coats-of-arms and has a later gadrooned edge. Like the fine screen surrounding it, the tomb was brought from the Bonhomme church at Ashridge in 1575, after the Dissolution. Similar, but badly defaced,

is the tomb with effigies of a knight and his lady in Kings Langley church, apparently to Sir Ralph Verney. This is also not in its original position but came, presumably, from the Dominican foundation which existed nearly till the Dissolution.

The most magnificent effigy is that in Ewelme church to Alice, grand-daughter of Chaucer and wife of William de la Pole, Earl of Suffolk, by whom this church was entirely rebuilt. The effigy, which has been cited as one of the very finest in the country, dating from 1475, is in alabaster surmounted by a magnificent canopy. On her left arm is the Order of the Garter, for she was one of the very few women of her time to be a member of the Order; there are only two other effigies in the country of women wearing it. The whole tomb is magnificently sculpted, and it has been restored, complete with much of its original colouring. The elaborate canopy behind her head is carved from a single block of stone. At the base of the tomb chest is an arcaded space containing a cadaver representing the Duchess at her death; on the ceiling of this chamber there are actually wall paintings (see 'Wall paintings').

BRASSES

The other great section of medieval monuments was the fascinating memorial brasses. A brass was a form of memorial by which a man of lesser wealth might perpetuate his name; brasses were introduced from the Continent in the late thirteenth century, and it would appear there are none earlier than 1280. In the Chilterns, the earliest dates from the early fourteenth century. The metal, which is finer quality brass, was all imported from the Continent and, in particular, from Cologne, whence originated 'Cullen Plate'. Because so much was imported, restrictions were imposed; this led to the peculiarly English custom of sinking the brasses in stone slabs. By this method a great deal of metal was saved. Nevertheless, a large quantity of brass went into the larger ones to men of importance; some of these exceed five feet in length. Yet the finest brasses produced in this country never attained the perfection achieved abroad.

It has been estimated that some 150,000 brasses were laid down in the middle ages, and a goodly number more up to about 1600; of all these some

Checkendon

Checkendon

30,000 have survived, though most are fragmentary.

There are many fine and interesting brasses to be found in the Chiltern churches. Of the more interesting examples is the fine, almost complete, brass, in Rotherfield Greys church, to a knight; compare this with a similarly complete brass, this time to a cleric, at Checkendon. The engraving of this figure pales, however, before the sheer magnificence of that in Edlesborough church. It has lost all its tracery, but the splendid figure commemorates John de Swynstede, who died in 1395, and was rector of the parish. Also in the same church is the unique 'Rose' brass, so called because it takes the form of a Tudor rose. Others are known to have existed but this is now the only one extant in the country. The inscription reads: 'What I spent, I have had; What I gave, I have; What I refused, I am being punished for; What I kept, I have lost.' The other inscription belongs to another brass.

At Checkendon church also there is a beautiful brass showing a soul being raised up by the angels.

At Aldbury, on the tomb chest of Sir Ralph Verney are brasses to himself, his wife and family; these date from 1546, shortly after the Reformation. Note therefore the elaboration of the dress, and, in particular, the ease of the stance, indicative of greater freedom to come.

Returning to other medieval brasses, there is a very fine but fragmentary collection at Chinnor. The peak of the English brass art was reached, as we have seen, in the fifteenth century; after the Reformation the art declined in favour of monumental sculpture, and may be said to have finally expired by the time of the Civil War.

At Chesham Bois is a minute brass to a chrysom child, Benedict, about 1550. 'Chrysom' implies that he died after baptism but before his mother had been churched, and he was buried in the cloth in which he had been anointed with chrysom at his baptism.

Almost as small is that to a young boy, John Drake, who died in 1623; the inscription reads:

Had hee liv'd to bee a man
This inch had grown but to a span.
Nowe is hee past all feare of paine,
'Twere sin to wish him heere againe.
Vewe but the way by wych wee come,
Thow't say hee's best that's first at home.

A truly delightful sentiment.

At Penn are a large number of brasses, all post-Reformation, and nearly all to members of the Penn family; an early one of 1540 shows a figure in a shroud. Note the elaborate engraving around the inscription. There is a much later brass of 1638 showing a family; but note the general poverty of the drawing and the design. This is, in fact, one of the very last in the Chilterns.

Before post-Reformation monuments, tomb recesses should be mentioned. It became a common practice in the fourteenth century to cut a recess in a wall to house a low tomb chest, and sometimes an effigy. Often the arches of these recesses were highly elaborated. There is a simple one at Burnham with traces of wall painting at the back.

Far more elaborate is that in Stoke Poges church; this dates from the mid fourteenth century and was erected to Sir John de Molyns, Marshal of the King's Falcons, and Supervisor of the King's Castles. Many more tomb recesses may be found.

One also comes across, from time to time, stone coffins, either in the church or in the churchyard, as at Northchurch, Hambleden, or in the churchyard at Ibstone. Some have been dug up during restorations in the churches; others from the churchyard. Apparently some were used as a kind of parish coffin.

Post-Reformation monuments present a formidable task to anyone studying them: they are so numerous. With the effigies there is a great change; away goes the recumbent effigy, and in its place appears the less pious kneeling figure, with eyes open bravely staring out into the face of death. There is far less humility about these effigies, and yet there is a greater realism which often generates a much greater feeling of tenderness and warmth of feeling, a greater sense of humanity than is evident in the medieval figure, all this particularly in the family groups. A fine example of this is the lovely Cope D'Oyley monument of about 1633, at Hambleden.

This is jumping ahead a little, however, for this raising of the figure did not take place immediately; recumbent figures continued in the medieval fashion till well into the seventeenth century. Thus there are the effigies of a man and his wife, with an almost identical pair opposite, in Lewknor church. And at Fulmer is the beautiful monument with effigies to Sir Marmaduke Dayrell and his wife, who died in 1631. He was the founder of this church. The whole monument has been well restored and re-coloured.

Tomb recesses also continued in use for some time; there is one of 1555, and another of 1572, both in Hambleden church.

Fulmer

Chesham

Half figures and busts became very popular in the early seventeenth century and these were generally placed in recesses in the wall, some distance from the floor. At Burnham is an early one of about 1594, to John Wright, sometime vicar, and another of about 1661 to George Evelyn of Huntercombe and his wife. There is a similar one at Sarratt to William Kingsley and his family, of about 1611, but the monument is wrongly dated 1502. Finally, there is the resplendent half figure to Richard Woodcoke, who died in 1623, at Chesham.

Reclining figures took the place of the medieval recumbent figures, and such a one is that at Ellesborough, to Bridget Croke, who died in 1638. This is a very large recessed monument and points the trend of monumental size.

Rotherfield Greys
The Knolly's tomb

Also of this large type, and seventeenth century, is the utterly superb Knolly's tomb at Rotherfield Greys, which is eminently worth its size. Here the figures are, for once, recumbent in the medieval fashion. All the decoration is very finely executed, and the whole monument was magnificently restored in 1960. The effigies are to Sir Francis Knollys and his wife and along each side kneel their children. He and his wife also kneel on top of the canopy in their ceremonial robes.

Rotherfield Greys
The Knolly's tomb

Besides the monuments which display a representation of the deceased there also appeared monuments of a purely decorative type, accompanied by an inscription. Such a one is that at Aldbury to Thomas Hyde and his son George, dating from about 1580. Note the strapwork around the skulls.

Skulls continued to prove a popular theme as in the elaborate marble plaque with rococo cartouche in The Lee church; this is to Thomas Plaistowe, *d* 1715. Another with a central skull theme is in Burnham church, and dates from 1707. Note the fine reserve of the decoration. There is also one at Stoke Poges with three skulls but no inscription.

This plaque type continued without skulls too, as in the remarkably lavish example at Stokenchurch, to Bartholomew Tipping, who died in 1680. The richness is typical of the period. There is also an eighteenth century one at Burnham, showing more reserve. The unusual plaque at Great Hampden was erected in the mid eighteenth century to the memory of John Hampden, the patriot, who was killed at the Battle of Chalgrove Field in 1643. This is said to be the only monument in a church which actually bears a battle-scene upon it.

The next two monuments, one from Lewknor, the other from Great Gaddesden church, are similar in style and date from the mid-eighteenth century. How different these are from the earlier bust type of memorial.

All the monuments considered so far, one will have noticed, bear the classical stamp. The Reformation virtually coincided with the introduction of renaissance architecture into this country. As the seventeenth century progressed, dedications became more verbose and vain, and the character of the figures and the whole monument more ostentatious and vainglorious. It was an attempt to impress the beholder, through the inscription, the decoration and the sheer size and grandeur of the monument, with the greatness of the deceased. The monument at Tring to Sir William Gore, who died in 1707, and was Lord Mayor of London, displays most of these attributes. It is ponderous and over ornate, and the typical poses display an air of contempt, even boredom. There are a series of equally heavy monuments at Amersham, including the interesting collection in the Drake chapel. As well, there is a monument to Henry Curwen, of Workington, of particularly early date, 1638. High Wycombe

Rotherfield Peppard

church besides being the largest in the Chilterns, and possessing the largest chest, may boast of the largest monument (excepting perhaps that in the Bedford Chapel at Chenies); this was erected in 1754 to Henry Petty, Earl of Shelburne, and was carved by the celebrated sculptor, Scheemakers. It is so large that there is no room really to comprehend it fully.

And so monuments progressed. The poses became freer, often fully standing, and contemptuous in death, and people delighted in being represented in classical drapes, and in classical attitudes of grief. In the nineteenth century this type of monument virtually ceased except in the rare cases of private chapels as at Lewknor, or Chenies, for example. The ordinary folk, or rather the middle class, had to be content with raising their statuary in the churchyard, and our yards and cemeteries bear full witness to this.

In the churchyards the eighteenth century provided many delightful rococo gravestones like those illustrated above from Rotherfield Peppard. On a more ambitious scale is the monument in Beaconsfield churchyard to Edmund Waller, the poet, who was locally born and bred and died in 1687.

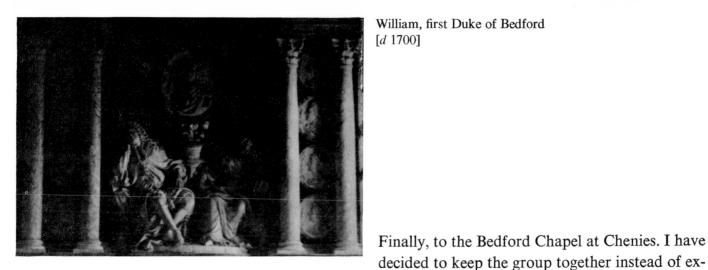

William, first Duke of Bedford
[d 1700]

Finally, to the Bedford Chapel at Chenies. I have decided to keep the group together instead of examining them separately because of their importance. All the monuments are housed in a private chapel attached to the church, and here are interred members of the Russell family of which the Duke of Bedford is the head. This remarkable collection is one of the finest in the country and includes examples of memorial sculpture from about 1560 right through to the present, though there are none of importance of this century. In this group one can witness in complete succession the gradual erection of the figure and the introduction of free statuary.

Francis, fourth Earl of Bedford
[d 1641]

Chesham

HATCHMENTS

Hatchments are simply the armorial bearings of the deceased, generally on lozenge-shaped wooden panels with a sable background, and were a survival of the practice of decorating the tombs of the dead with their helms, shields and other accoutrements of war. This, in itself, was probably a lingering reminder of the primitive belief that the dead would need food, weapons and suchlike in the after life as witnessed in the burial chambers of pre-history. Helms can be seen in the churches at Fulmer, Stoke Poges and Berkhamsted as relics of this custom, which ceased towards the end of the seventeenth century. By then, any personal protection was no longer effective against the well established firearm. But the arms of war, if not existing in fact, continued to be represented, incorporated in the permanent decoration of a monument; a particular example of this is the monument in St Leonard's church to Cornelius Wood, one of Queen Anne's lieutenant-generals, who died in 1712. The use of hatchments and the old practice of using the accoutrements of the deceased overlapped considerably for here also, as late as 1712, above the monument, is the funeral helm with its crest, and gauntlets.

It was probably the mid-seventeenth century that saw the last upsurge of a custom which but for the Civil War might have ceased earlier. Even then the shield as a practical defence had not been used for well over one hundred years, but the shield continued to be used to display arms. Somewhere, therefore, in between, the hatchment usurped the shield, but its true development is obscure. Did the lozenge-shape derive from similarly shaped jousting shields of the mid sixteenth century? Or did it originate from a square framed canvas or board? And might it have been the ladies who first prompted their production, since they themselves could not rightly employ an ordinary war shield? All that is certain is that hatchments were in general use by the early eighteenth century. They were sometimes on canvas like an oil painting; even embroidered banners were hung over the tombs. These are still in use, as are even shields of arms and mock helms as may be seen hanging over the family seats of the Viscount Wendover in High Wycombe church.

Hatchments tell, by complex heraldic devices, exactly whose arms they bear, and that person's lineage. The custom was to hang a hatchment outside the house when the bearer died and then, after several months, to hang it in the church over the deceased's tomb. Even in the nineteenth century when tombs and memorials of any size ceased to be erected and entombments within the church generally stopped, hatchments continued to be hung. The last in the Chilterns, apparently, are two members of the Fuller family in Chesham Bois church dating from 1882 and 1892. The earliest, peculiarly enough, is that of a woman, Anne Borlase, in Medmenham church; it dates from her death in 1677, and is even more remarkable because it so small. Also in the same church is a nineteenth century example. Chesham has many hatchments in the south transept, now the vestry; and there are others in the churches at Fulmer, Penn, Stoke Poges and Hemel Hempstead. All of these are eighteenth or nineteenth century and hatchments no longer appear to be employed anywhere except in very rare instances.

PULPITS

The message of Christianity was spread at first by missionaries preaching in town and village squares, and by the wayside. Because of the difficulties of celebrating mass, preaching took on extra importance; but with the establishment of permanent places of worship, mass came into its own again in the late Saxon and Norman periods. Then, in the mid fourteenth century, preaching became very popular again largely due to Wycliffe and his Lollard sect, to the introduction of vernacular bibles, and, indirectly, to the great changes brought by the Black Death. Even so, ceremony remained paramount till the Reformation in the sixteenth century.

The very earliest pulpits surviving are of stone and date from no earlier than about 1380, about the earliest any were made at all; few have survived. The majority were of wood, but, of these, it is very dubious if any exist from before the fifteenth century. Those of the fifteenth century were usually octagonal, with cusped and traceried panelling, and finials at the angles, often painted and gilded in their day, and generally very finely carved. When the Reformation took place these pulpits generally survived, though not untouched, basically because preaching was the great panacea of the new church, the antidote to the superstition and idolatry that went before.

Ibstone church, small and remote, tucked away in the heart of the hills, is fortunate in possessing an early fifteenth century oak pulpit, dark with age, with two traceried panels on each face separated by small pinnacled buttresses. If this pulpit originally belonged here, what a delight this building must once have been, now, alas, so dark and plain.

Edlesborough

The better pulpits all had sounding boards, or testers, over them, but only about six medieval ones survive. Edlesborough's pulpit with its tester is, perhaps, the finest in the country, and it would be interesting to discover how it has survived. Not surprisingly, it is the glory of the church and an outstanding example of fifteenth century work. The pulpit, which is of oak, as was most medieval woodwork, is octagonal, with two sides forming the door; the whole is raised on an octagonal shaft with curved ribs. At the angles are buttresses and crocketed finials, while the faces have sunk panels with elaborately cusped and traceried heads, and brackets for images. These latter were, of course, destroyed at the Reformation. At the back there is no proper standard, only two posts supporting the tester, or canopy, which soars upwards in three diminishing stages, crowned by an openwork spire. The whole is highly elaborate and a magnificent conception of the woodworker's art.

Of pulpits prior to the Reformation, those at Ibstone and Edlesborough are the only examples in the Chilterns. After the Reformation, very little new work was carried out till the early seventeenth century, when pulpits were ordered to be erected by James I; also, by then, the changes brought by the Reformation had settled down into a pattern. The Jacobean period, the late middle ages and the mid eighteenth century, are the three periods when pulpit design and construction attained great heights. But it is the Jacobean which was not only most prolific in its output, by order, but from which most survive; and the Chiltern churches have a very fair share.

The pulpit at King's Langley is perhaps the greatest achievement of this period in the Chilterns; it is hexagonal in shape, complete with standard and original tester, with all surfaces carved and panelled in the Jacobean manner. The wood colour is an unusual orange-brown, in contrast to the very dark brown of oak of which most pulpits were made, and it would be interesting to discover whether this is due to the wood employed or to subsequent restoration.

Almost as good is the hexagonal pulpit at Pitstone, again complete with standard and tester, all very elaborately panelled and carved. The soffit of the tester is panelled and has turned drops, while the wall standard supporting it is flanked by pierced scrolls.

Yet another complete example of the early seventeenth century is close by in Ivinghoe church. This also is hexagonal, as opposed to the medieval octagon, and of oak, elaborately panelled and enriched with strapwork though all the details are somewhat cruder than on other pulpits. The lower panel of the standard is interesting because it is crudely carved with a representation of the Resurrection.

Also following the normal pattern and surviving intact is that at Sarratt which is raised on a stalk or central stem.

All the other early seventeenth century pulpits, of

Kings Langley

which there are several, have had their testers removed, generally during the nineteenth century, when even whole pulpits of the period were thrown out. Chesham Bois pulpit is worth noting because of the use made of the tester: it now serves as the base. The pulpit itself follows the usual pattern: hexagonal body of oak, panelled and carved with good strapwork and openwork. That at Princes Risborough is similar.

The pulpit at Little Kimble church, not far away, has the distinction of being square with simply carved panels of the early seventeenth century. It is possible that the pulpit has been made up from old panels rather than being completely original.

A good example recording the nineteenth century destruction of earlier pulpits is to be found in the panels of Medmenham's pulpit. These panels, which are of the early seventeenth century, are carved with representations of the Nativity, and the Annuciation, and originally belonged to the three decker pulpit which apparently existed till the restoration of 1839. Whether this three decker was also of the seventeenth century will probably remain a mystery, but if so it would have been one of the very first, for three deckers really belong exclusively to the eighteenth century. Per-

haps a Jacobean pulpit was converted; thus the panels.

The Civil War and subsequent Commonwealth brought an abrupt halt to all Jacobean work, and much destruction. Many surviving medieval pulpits must have disappeared at this time, and even some later ones in the midst of indiscriminate pillage.

After the Restoration, the building of pulpits never resumed its former zest, largely because the prolific production of the Jacobeans had fulfilled most requirements, and few new churches were built outside London till the eighteenth century. Only where pulpits had been destroyed or badly damaged were new ones made.

Examples of this period are to be found at Radnage, a late seventeenth century hexagonal pulpit on a turned shaft, and at Great Hampden. Undoubtedly the best of the period is that at Fawley, which is not of local origin but came from the chapel at Canons, the great mansion at Little Stanmore, Middlesex, built by the Duke of Chandos, when it was pulled down in 1747. The pulpit is hexagonal and of oak, and even if not by Grinling Gibbons, as has been suggested, is still an excellent product of the time, dating from about 1700.

All these post Restoration pulpits are marked out from their Jacobean counterparts by finer and more restrained carving, though they lack the earlier exuberance.

The eighteenth century saw the rise of the short lived three decker pulpits consisting of pulpit, lectern and clerk's seat. These were probably introduced to raise the parson high enough to command attention from those people in the newly built galleries and those esconced in high walled pews, sometimes complete with fireplaces. Very few pulpits of this type survive because they were a particular target of the Victorian reformer; they were rendered obsolete by the removal of high pews and galleries, and, to some extent, represented all that was wrong with the indolent eighteenth century church.

In the Chilterns the only eighteenth century pulpits are those at Rotherfield Peppard, and in the strange church at West Wycombe converted by Sir Francis Dashwood, in 1763, from a medieval structure to the height of contemporary fashion. This pulpit may well be unique, for it is in the form of a desk so that the parson could sit and sermonize. There is also a later pulpit there, which may be late eighteenth century, simply panelled and on a high central stem.

Fawley

When the nineteenth century zealots destroyed great numbers of earlier pulpits and replaced them with ones more compatible with their credo, few can doubt their sincerity, but more can doubt the taste displayed in most of these replacements, particularly the stone types raised in admiration of the Gothic.

One of their better works is that in Little Gaddesden church which dates from about 1880 and is strongly reminiscent of the work of G. F. Watts; the imagery represents the attempt to recapture the mystery of the medieval church.

All together then, the pulpits of so small an area as the Chilterns form a highly adequate representative collection, equally adequate in the quality of their design.

Within this framework of the spreading of the word, one must also place the lectern and the less frequently occurring reading desk. Very few medieval lecterns remain anywhere, but that in Bledlow church, of dark oak and simply carved in the familiar eagle form, which was copied later in the ubiquitous brass type which is the bane of so many churches, may well be fifteenth century. There is an Elizabethan one in Ivinghoe church which has a double top, revolving on an octagonal shaft. All other lecterns appear to be of the nineteenth century except one at Fawley, brought from Canons like all the other woodwork there. There is an eighteenth century reading desk in West Wycombe church matching the desk pulpit, but these desks were a peculiarly eighteenth century device, of which the Victorians would have no part, with the usual consequences.

SCREENS

Chinnor

The most important screen that occurs, or occurred, in any church is that separating nave and chancel, temporal and spiritual – the rood or chancel screen; other surviving screens generally enclose chapels, often family ones, or tombs, and are termed 'parclose'. From as early as the seventh century a screen and a rood, that is a crucifix, marked this dividing line in the church; this was a very real division in the early medieval period, for the chancel was the property of the priest, or more usually his patron, and the nave belonged to the parishioners. This system gradually broke down to a point where, as today, the church was considered as a single unit. This is particularly evident by the fifteenth century when new churches were built without chancel arches, and old arches were sometimes removed. However, a screen and a rood were still erected right across the church, not to distinguish whose property was whose but to maintain the division between priest and parishioner, and to maintain the mystery of the mass, which could hardly have been comprehended by the medieval layman.

There are no screens of importance earlier than the thirteenth century, if any exist at all. Even thirteenth century ones are rare; they are quite simple in design and tend to imitate stone architectural forms in wood. The Chilterns are more than fortunate in posessing an example in Chinnor church; this dates from *c* 1250, being Early English in character, and clumsily imitates stone forms in oak.

These screens grew richer and more elaborate, reaching a peak of magnificence in the late fifteenth century, with foliage and figures painted, carved, and gilded. Many, of course, fell short of this but were still rich and costly. The roods, with their attendant figures of Saints Mary and John, grew equally rich and were even draped with expensive materials and precious ornaments; and with this increasing personification of the figures came superstition and rife reports of miracles 'before the rood'. The Wendover Rood became so famous that pilgrimages were made there, and as late as 1506, as a punishment, several townspeople of Chesham were ordered to make a journey to this rood. What had begun as symbols and as works to the greater glory of God became idolatrous and one of the great evils of the late medieval church.

The rood loft, which was a gangway along the top of the screen, reached by stairs often cut in a pier as at Edlesborough, seems to have been introduced in the fourteenth century and subsequently enriched and elaborated. The gospels were read, apparently, from this loft, and candles were kept burning constantly there before the rood. This feverish adulation of the rood is indicated in many ways, thus by the enrichment of the roof immediately above it as at Ivinghoe (see 'Roofs'), and the insertion elsewhere of much larger windows on the south side to light it better; and, above all, by the extreme attention of the reformers in pulling down all the roods and burning them. They were not all burnt at the time because many were erected again, together with many other 'forbidden' appointments, during the short Marian interlude, but the last must have disappeared in the reign of Elizabeth. That the destruction was zealously executed finally is illustrated by the fact that not one survives. It is said that the Wendover Rood survived till 1842 but more probably it was the rood-screen

Swyncombe
loft and screen

Several churches now possess modern roods, some the result of the Victorian 'Gothick' movement, while others have been erected this century, generally as war memorials. The Chilterns have two examples of this at Bledlow and Saunderton, churches, note well, only a few miles apart. Of the nineteenth century roods there are examples at Amersham and Bradenham; a variation occasionally occurs like the rood painted above the chancel arch at Tring. These roods are no longer associated with the superstition and dread horrors of the medieval hereafter.

When the roods were pulled down most lofts were also destroyed, or at least badly damaged; then the majority of those disappeared during the Commonwealth or during the nineteenth century with the screens. There are modern examples, which no longer have any function, at Tring and Swyncombe. Many rood screens survived the first onslaught, generally to suffer from the zealots of the nineteenth century before the 'Gothick' movement had fully gained control. Many would have been damaged by the removal or destruction of lofts, or images whether painted or carved; possibly the greatest number of screens were damaged or destroyed during the Civil War and the Commonwealth, as happened to so many other fittings. In Berkhamsted church is a fifteenth century screen which has had its figures restored, giving some idea of its former glory; it is now used as a reredos to the main altar.

Of surviving painted screens, that at Monks Risborough is the only example in the Chilterns with

onks Risborough

Edlesborough

figure work; the nine strange figures, once medieval, were repainted probably in the late seventeenth or early eighteenth centuries. There is some controversy as to whom they represent and why there are only nine, with three empty panels. The most likely reason is that originally there were twelve figures representing the Apostles. The fact that no traces of painting exist on the other three panels does not signify very much. Otherwise this screen has been restored with new tracery in the spandrels. Other painted screens do exist, but with patterns, and they were repainted during nineteenth century restorations; it is unknown what foundation there is for the authenticity of these patterns and colours. There are two of this type, both very fine screens in themselves, at High Wycombe and Edlesborough. The former was first erected in 1468 by Richard Redehode of that town, as a parclose screen, and removed in 1563. However, in 1895 the fragments were carefully restored and re-erected. The original dedicatory inscription is worth noting: 'Pray ye for the Soulys of Rychard Redehode, Agnes hys wyfe, ther son Willm et Johan hys wyfe. (Rychard bilded thys) p(ar)clos (with tymbre in the yere off oure Lord God MCCCCLXVIII, on whos Soulys have mercy God)'.

The screen at Edlesborough, which is well traceried, is also of the fifteenth century, like the magnificent pulpit there. It is exceptionally fine, though still not to be compared with the screens of Devon or East Anglia. It is of great interest that here the gates survive, for all medieval screens originally had them; the loft has long since disappeared although part of the coving still exists on the east side.

Other medieval screens exist at Ewelme, Horsenden and Beaconsfield, while there are nineteenth century examples at Wooburn, Tring, Amersham, Bradenham, and Swyncombe, and elsewhere, and one at Bledlow contemporary with the rood mentioned earlier. There is still some mystery why so many screens survived the Reformation at all, but they conveniently cut off the chancel which had little part to perform in the rituals of the reformed church, and they were suitable supports for the newly ordered royal coats-of-arms.

Stone screens are even rarer, for several reasons: this is not a good stone area, so there would have been a tendency, in screens to enclose side chapels or tombs, to use wood unless sufficient money was forthcoming; and as for stone rood screens, they are extremely rare anywhere. In fact, only one stone screen, a parclose, exists in the Chilterns, at Aldbury. This is particularly fine but did not originally belong to the church; it came from the church of the Bonhomme community at Ashridge, close by, after the dissolution of the monasteries. This screen, which encloses two sides of the Whittingham tomb and includes a low entrance doorway to the chapel, is a very good example of late fifteenth century tracery work and may well be of local stone from the Pitstone or Totternhoe quarries.

There are, then, in the Chiltern churches, few early screens, and fewer of particular merit, but considering past history it is not so surprising: the Chilterns were never very wealthy, and the most ornate screens would have been the major targets of the reformers, particularly in an area such as this where a strong streak of non-conformism and Puritanism has long persisted.

OTHER WOODWORK

Ivinghoe

Besides screens, wood was employed for a large number of other appointments in a church, such as in pulpits and lecterns, and roofs, which are considered separately. Otherwise wood was used most notably for seating.

In the early middle ages there was little or no seating accommodation in church; people stood, or sat on small stone ledges along the walls or around columns. But by the late fourteenth century, or the early fifteenth century, most churches were completely fitted out with pews of oak, often decorated in a vernacular manner. Not many exist in the Chilterns, mainly because the carving of bench ends and pew heads never reached that stage which would have prevented their wholesale destruction in the nineteenth century. There is some fifteenth century work with poppyheads

at Edlesborough, about four well carved figure pew heads at Monks Risborough, and a real forest of pew heads carved with faces, men and mermaids at Ivinghoe.

More illustrious seating is to be found in the chancel where there are the stalls. Only a handful have survived from the middle ages; in the Chilterns they only exist at Edlesborough. Like all stalls of the period they face east and are fixed to the east side of the screen. Under the seats are a series of fine fifteenth century misericords carved with every conceivable figure of a whimsical nature.

Of later years, there are the eighteenth century box pews, as at Penn, but most have disappeared along with the galleries and manorial pews of the period. There are also the sickly varnished pitch

Edlesborough

pine pews of the nineteenth century which are seen all too frequently.

In a number of churches, usually in the chancel, one will come across an upright chair or two, dating from the seventeenth or eighteenth centuries. Some are used as bishops' thrones, or for the incumbent; some were specifically designed for their purpose, others are ordinary domestic chairs. Of the former there is a massive seventeenth century throne at Amersham and a very fine gilded bishop's throne of the late seventeenth century at Beaconsfield. There are ordinary chairs at Chalfont St Giles, Great Hampden, Hughenden and elsewhere.

Other woodwork may be found in the form of panelling, as at Fawley, where it was all brought from Canons, Little Stanmore, in Middlesex, in 1747; or at Burnham where the north transept is completely panelled with some fine carved work of foreign origin, with scenes from the life of Jesus, and other various decoration. Although modern panelling is rare, there is some pleasing oak work in the sanctuary at Little Missenden dating from after World War I.

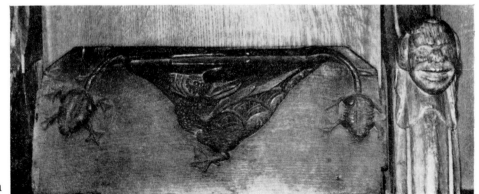

Edlesborough

ROOFS

Henley

Medieval church roofs are among the great glories of the English parish church; their variety is endless. Over twenty of the Chiltern churches have old roofs of interest. Penn roof, which is a fine steep pitched type, dates from about 1400, and there are two fine traceried solid tie beam roofs of the fifteenth century at Great Missenden and Radnage. Totternhoe nave roof dates from the same period and has decorated beams. More elaborate, and very fine, is the nave roof at Ivinghoe, with its angels. The most elaborate part is the rood celure, directly over where the rood would have stood (see 'Screens'). The angel roof in St John's Chapel at Ewelme is perhaps the loveliest of all in the Chilterns; it owes much to the East Anglian tradition.

Later roofs were rarely decorated, until the nineteenth century. Then there was a vogue for painted beams and painted panelled ceilings, particularly in the chancels. These often reveal better taste than is usual in nineteenth century church art; instance the chancel roofs at Henley, Beaconsfield, Tring, and Hambleden, redecorated in 1953.

82

CHESTS

Beaconsfield

Chests, throughout all spheres of medieval life, were virtually a type of universal furniture and, as such, were extremely important. They were no less important to the church, for they were used for the vestments of the clergy, to hold the parish records (as many still do today), to keep safely the parochial funds, and to house the vast collections of 'relics', plate, sacramental vessels, and all the acquisitions of centuries of giving by a people to whom both God and the devil were vividly real. Despite the apparent misconception that each church had only one chest, most had two or more, and not small either; many of those today that have survived would not have held one tenth of the possessions of an average medieval church. The fact that few possess more than one today, if that, is because many chests

83

became redundant when the churches were despoiled, and so were disposed of, or disappeared under the hand of the restorer. Otherwise these chests exist in an abundance, of all shapes, sizes and materials, because of their essentially practical and secular functions.

The Chilterns possess some twenty or so chests, all medieval or, more commonly, renaissance, because the numbers then produced more than satisfied later requirements. The fact that the majority date from after the Reformation may be attributed to a desire for some sophistication hardly evident in the early crude slab chests still surviving then. For the most part these Chiltern chests are plain and simple, as at Bradenham, which is of panelled oak dating from the seventeenth century; at Burnham, an iron-bound example of about 1600; at Chalfont St Peter, two of the seventeenth century; at Chenies, a seventeenth century carved oak chest; two at Edlesborough, one dated 1689; two at Great Gaddesden, one carved out of a solid log; and the chests at Lewknor and Hemel Hempstead which are similar types, very heavily bound with iron, dating from the fourteenth or fifteenth centuries.

The immense robust specimen of an iron bound type at Little Gaddesden is so plain that it could just as well be sixteenth or seventeenth century. That in Great Kimble church is long and low, of oak bound with slightly decorated ironwork, and could be fourteenth century. Another iron bound chest, but much larger and similar to that at Little Gaddesden, stands in Kings Langley church and may be fifteenth or sixteenth century. Tring church also possesses two iron bound chests, but neither is of any distinction. The chest at Wooburn, though plain in its body, has richly carved feet and has been assigned a date as early as the late thirteenth century. High Wycombe, besides being the largest church in Buckinghamshire, can also boast of the largest chest in the Chilterns, probably sixteenth century, and of oak. The 'Pitstone Chest' at the church of that name is one of the more distinguished ones, being of an unusual design: it is iron bound, with curiously carved feet, and is fitted with no fewer than three locks. There was a good reason for this: the three keys were distributed, one to the priest and one each to the two church-wardens. The chest could only be opened when all three were present, thus any misappropriation of the funds was prevented. Some of the other chests illustrated also have three locks or padlocks. Pitstone chest probably dates from the late thirteenth or fourteenth centuries.

In comparison that in Beaconfield church is much finer. It is an iron framed chest, almost certainly seventeenth century, which is panelled and painted with small scenes and landscapes.

Northchurch

The finest by far, however, and possibly among the finest in the country of its period, is the chest at Northchurch, which is a superb example of fifteenth century work, being panelled and carved with rich tracery and shafts and pinnacles, and is fastened by a good lock and wrought iron plate. It is, not surprisingly, not of local workmanship but apparently Flemish, possibly imported, or perhaps executed by immigrants. This chest more than compensates for the simplicity of most other chests, which are just so all over England, and must be regarded as one of the great treasures of the Chiltern churches.

WALL PAINTINGS

The mention of wall paintings usually conjures up for modern man a picture of red devils tormenting souls in hell, and fantasies out of the pictures of Hieronimus Bosch; but this is only a narrow judgment of but one era – the Gothic. Wall paintings, admittedly, are usually associated with this period in particular but the field is really wider. In the history of the English parish church there are five periods of wall painting: the late Romanesque or Norman, the Gothic, the post-Reformation period and the seventeenth century, the eighteenth century, and the Victorian era. The twentieth century appears to have little or no place for mural decoration in its churches.

Unlike Italian murals, which were generally frescoes in the true sense – that is, the pigment was applied directly on to wet plaster – English wall paintings were executed in tempera. The pigment was bound with a medium and applied to the dry plastered walls. Colours were few and mainly of an earth origin; blacks, blues, greens and yellows do appear in these paintings, and red is predominant, being an easily obtainable earth pigment. The other colours may have been used more frequently than would appear from what survives, for the red used was particularly durable.

There is little or no record of pre-Conquest painting, but under Norman rule the art began to flourish. In this period wall painting seems to have followed the same course as all other decoration; for almost the first hundred years decoration of any kind was kept to a minimum and very simple. Then followed a rapid development, leading through the transitional period to the glorious outbursts of the Early English style. Few wall paintings can be dated earlier than 1150; at that time common forms of decoration were masonry patterns, multi-coloured stripes, stars, dado scrolls, diapering, and the inevitabe consecration crosses. There are good examples at Little Missenden of dado work, masonry and stripes; good diapering, dado and stars in the apse at Swyncombe, and consecration crosses, which also occur at Penn, Radnage and Little Missenden. All these designs, although liberally

Little Missenden
St Christopher

applied, were strictly conventional and follow the same geometrical theme as in the stone carving of the period.

Then, sometime in the early thirteenth century, figures began to appear, accompanied by a similar release in other decoration, such as the appearance of stiff, undercut foliage on capitals. But the designs remained stiff and stylized. The St Christopher in Little Hampden church epitomizes this, and dates from the early thirteenth century; this very early painting has a further but unconfirmed distinction, for it is claimed that this is the earliest surviving representation of St Christopher in the country. Actually, the figure has been dated as late thirteenth century but if it is to be regarded as the earliest then it must predate that at Little Missenden, and appearances would tend to confirm this. The Little Missenden St Christopher is particularly fine and remarkable for its completeness, and is very striking to anyone just entering the church. This relationship to the entrance is generally common to all St Christophers. The story of the saint ferrying the Christ child across a river first appeared in a German poem of the twelfth century. Because of this, he became the patron saint of travellers and was painted on a wall where he might be seen by any traveller looking in, usually on a north wall facing the south entrance. The medieval attitude is best expressed thus: 'He who today has seen St Christopher shall be free from the assault of illness and sudden death'. Perhaps because of this wide patronage he was the most portrayed saint

Little Kimble
*burial of St Catherine,
and St Benedict*

of all, and it has been calculated that some two hundred representations of him remain today. If this is accurate then the Chilterns with their small number of churches ought to have, on average, only one; in fact there are seven. These include the two already mentioned, another fragmentary fifteenth century one at Little Hampden; one of the early fourteenth century at Little Kimble; a very faint example at Bledlow: one in similar condition and in the south aisle, at Chesham; and the top half only at Radnage.

To return to the development of wall painting, the mass of paintings at Little Missenden are by far the most representative of early work in the area, if not further afield. Besides the St Christopher, there is a series of panels, of which five remain, showing the Passion of St Catherine of Alexandria, of the same date, *c* 1280-1300. St Catherine was a popular figure in the medieval period, and there is a scene showing her burial on Mount Sinai, at Little Kimble, above the south door; this dates from about 1300. There are

Little Kimble
St George

also scenes from her life on the south wall of the south aisle in Chalfont St Giles church, dating from *c* 1330. Even earlier paintings at Little Missenden are a fine 'Crucifixion', faced by an 'Annunciation', and, on the south wall of the nave, fragments of a 'Passion', all mid thirteenth century.

Of the fourteenth century, there are a mass of excellent early examples at Little Kimble, among the best in Buckinghamshire, and in the Chilterns, though many are only fragmentary. To the west of the burial of St Catherine is a splendid patriarchal figure that is thought to be St Benedict; and on the east and west walls are many indecipherable fragments. The best, however, are on the north wall and include what is held to be a history of St Margaret, and many saints such as St Francis of Assisi, possibly a St James, and a magnificent St George. St George became one of the most popular saints, second to the Virgin; he appeared in a vision to the crusaders at the siege of Antioch in 1098 and was then revered until he superseded St Edward the Confessor as the national saint from the early fourteenth century onwards.

There are many good fragments of fourteenth century work at Radnage; those in the nave are almost entirely indistinguishable, but there are good figures on the east wall of the chancel which include Christ in Majesty with the Virgin and the Archangel Gabriel, two Old and two New Testament saints. A similar display, but eminently finer, occurs in the apse at Checkendon church.

The Penn doom

Here again is Christ in Majesty but with Peter and Paul flanking him because they are the patron saints of this church. The rest of the Apostles are arrayed on either side. These paintings are difficult to date, but from the general style, the formalized poses and the mystical elongation of the figures, they could well be of the late thirteenth century, or, at the latest, the early fourteenth century. Elsewhere there are very few instances of paintings surviving in the chancel; but at Abbots Langley, high up on the east wall of the south chapel, are two restored figures of the mid fourteenth century representing Saints Thomas and Lawrence.

Other fourteenth century work includes a Christ in Majesty of about 1340 in a tomb recess at Little Missenden; an Adam and Eve, and other fragments, at Bledlow; and many fragments at Little Hampden. The largest series of the fourteenth century are the prolific medley of paintings on the south wall of the south aisle at Chalfont St Giles, dating from about 1330. These include the life of St Catherine of Alexandria, scenes from Genesis, and the lives of the Virgin and Christ. Unfortunately they are all indistinct, but careful reconstructions by Professor Tristram are displayed beneath the originals.

Of all medieval wall painting the most important was the doom, or last judgment, the dominating theme of the medieval church. This represented the last day when all would be judged and condemned to hell or received into heaven; it usually consisted of Christ in Majesty with apostles and angels, the Archangel Michael weighing souls while the devil attempts to tip the scales, the Virgin interceding for lost souls, and, inevitably, souls burning in hell. Naturally because of its importance, the doom occupied a dominating position, usually above the chancel arch. There are fragments of one at Little Missenden, and one on the south wall at Little Hampden. The prize of the Chilterns is the doom at Penn, which is unusual in being painted on oak boards which were orignally fastened above the chancel arch. Even more incredible is that it has survived, for the boards were discovered in a heap in 1938 and very ably reassembled, cleaned and restored by Clive Rouse. It is certainly one of the richest in colouring of surviving English dooms, but considering the date of the painting, two periods, early and late fifteenth century, it is not of great artistic merit. The earlier is the better, dating from about 1400-1410, and of which there are only traces, including a fine St Michael. The later painting was superimposed about 1480.

By the fifteenth century there was much more freedom in the poses of the figures, and in their gesture and movement, and even the beginnings of realism and pictorial composition. All this was in keeping with the general trend in the ways of the church, of the increasingly affluent society, and as shown in other aspects of the arts.

With the increasing use of stained glass with its glowing colour, the play of light, shade and hue, and the technical improvements in architecture, during the fifteenth century there was a move away from wall painting as a communicative medium and towards stained glass, windows occupying much of what earlier would have been walls. Painting was, of course, still liberally employed but no longer as the dominating decorative feature, except in the less wealthy churches as in the Chilterns where few large windows were inserted and new churches of the period were rare. One such new church was Ewelme, entirely rebuilt except for the tower, with much window space; yet wall painting still found a place. On the walls of the south chapel are restored fifteenth century IHS monograms, painted niches and corbels, but no representation figures. One tends to think of such decoration more in the post-Reformation era, but it really is simple wall decoration as a complement to the new status of stained glass.

Also in the same church, underneath the fabulous tomb to Alice, Duchess of Suffolk, in the arcaded space below the tomb chest, were found several rough paintings.

In the Chiltern churches there are other remnants of medieval wall painting at Sarratt and Great Missenden, and some is known to exist but as yet uncovered at The Lee; much more must also remain uncovered in other churches. All these fragments give an overall idea of medieval mural painting and lead to the amazing realisation that literally everything was painted, including window jambs, porches and even fonts, and every spare inch of wall space. Medieval wall paintings bear a marked resemblance to contemporary

Ewelme

illuminated manuscripts and it must be considered that these, in fact, were the models issued to the painters, or at least used as a basis. It is also important to realise that although these mural paintings were the 'People's Bible', they were propaganda, admittedly occasioned by illiteracy, and interpretations of the scriptures. Not surprisingly, when Wycliffe's Bible and other translations appeared and were read by literates these interpretations were disputed, thus sowing the seeds of the Reformation and non-conformism.

The Reformation quickly put an end to what was considered blasphemous imagery, and all the paintings were rapidly covered with plaster or whitewash; moralizing texts were then profusely applied. Over the chancel arches, where the dooms originally were, appeared by order, the Ten Commandments, the creed, and the Lord's Prayer, as at Chalfont St Giles, and later at Pitstone, in 1733. Texts continued to be painted till well into the eighteenth century. Many have disappeared, along with countless medieval wall paintings, or in the search for the earlier work, but examples can be found at Bledlow in profusion, The Lee, Radnage, Fawley, Penn, and elsewhere. Despite the abhorrence of imagery, there still appears to have been a need for illustrating the meaning of the texts, otherwise the texts credit the people of the period with an amazing literacy; thus at Hedgerley is a very unusual seventeenth century framed canvas with the Ten Commandments illustrated and explained! Only in more sophisticated circles was imagery really acceptable, and more so generally as the eighteenth century progressed, particularly in new buildings; hence the dome of St Paul's Cathedral, or, in the Chilterns, the chancel ceiling of West Wycombe church. This was the church completely classicized by the much maligned Sir Francis Dashwood, founder of the Dilettanti Society and the notorious Hell Fire Club. This painting is a fine version of the 'Last Supper', by Borgnis, about 1765. The rest of the church is sumptuously stuccoed and painted.

The religious revival of the Victorian era brought a new interest in wall painting and many new texts were painted, as at Chesham; but there was, as well, a release from the 'ban' on imagery. Many scenes were painted like the 'Crucifixion' over Tring chancel arch, that above Henley chancel arch, and the fine painting in the same position at Aldbury by an Italian artist in about 1900. At Little Gaddesden, the east wall of the chancel is lavishly decorated and even the steps are coloured in the manner of the revived symbolism of the period.

It was also during the same period that most earlier wall paintings were destroyed through rebuilding, repair, or through the belief in the desirability of bare stone walls, as at Ellesborough and Stoke Poges. But, of course, many wall paintings were already irretrievably damaged through the neglect of the eighteenth century and the consequent ruinous state of the walls. Since the turn of the century there has been little desire or demand for wall decoration, except in the restoration of that existing or in the search for medieval work, or occasionally in the new churches.

STAINED GLASS

Most people are aware of the wonder of medieval stained glass; it is a legend, and rightly so.

The Chiltern churches, unfortunately, have only the barest fragments left after the depredations of the past. There is, probably, only one complete window, a tiny gem no more than a foot high, at Edlesborough. This shows a pilgrim who, from the scallop shell in his hat, had evidently visited the shrine of St James of Compostella. Also one must not forget the famous 'Bicycle Window' at Stoke Poges, which is named after the fragment showing a figure blowing a trumpet and riding an ancient hobby horse. Nearly all the other medieval glass consists of fragments of patterns which only survived because they were inoffensive to the iconoclasts, or were out of reach in the window tracery.

There is an appreciable amount of sixteenth, seventeenth, and eighteenth century glass to be found. At Medmenham are four good sixteenth century roundels which were presented to the church in 1839; they represent the death and Ascension of Christ. And at Fulmer are four German or Flemish roundels depicting the four Petrarch Triumphs. At West Wycombe the whole east window of the chancel is filled with seventeenth century glass of a monotone type favoured then. There is some sixteenth century heraldic glass at Turville, and some very fine early eighteenth century glass, also of a heraldic nature. The east window of Amersham chancel glows with seventeenth century foreign glass brought there in 1760 from the private chapel at Lamer in Hertfordshire.

The majority of stained glass is, of course, Victorian, and that is about all that can be said about it. The Victorians tried to revive the magic of medieval glass but produced, only too often, a hideousness of colour that is the death of many interiors. Otherwise, Victorian glass is an immense subject which demands an exhaustive study to separate the wheat from the chaff, and to establish some sort of perspective view of it. Twentieth century glass does not occur very often, because not only are few people willing or able to make such donations nowadays, but most of the windows are full already. Where there is any it generally has a nineteenth century flavour in its colour and form.

TILES

Little Kimble
two of the Chertsey tiles

Clay tiles formed one of the major floor coverings of the middle ages; since then they have only been widely utilized during the nineteenth century. At first, floors were simply beaten earth strewn with rushes or straw; then slabs of stone were laid. Many of the Chiltern churches must have remained without such solid floors because of the difficulty and expense of carting suitable flags from Oxfordshire or Northamptonshire. Stone certainly was brought to the area, and in immense quantities, but from the number of tiles surviving and their obviously extensive use, tiles were evidently considered a good alternative. The availability of brick earth was an influencing factor; this was at hand and occurs in pockets all over the Chilterns, particularly in the eastern half. To an extent, this accounts for the floor of old Flaunden church being entirely covered; these

tiles, which probably date from the fourteenth century and bear common patterns in singles and fours, were transferred last century to the new church. This is not to say that churches that could obtain suitable stone ignored tiles as a flooring medium; all recognised their decorative potentialities.

The earliest tiles probably date from the early thirteenth century; for the most part they were plain or decorated with very simple patterns, which grew more ambitious, extending even to representations of figures and little scenes from legends and the scriptures. The best of this latter type are the six Chertsey tiles in Little Kimble church, which date from the late thirteenth century and presumably came, somehow, from Chertsey Abbey. The incidents portrayed come from

95

Horsenden

the story of Tristram and Iseult and show a king on a throne, a man giving a book to a woman, a knight charging, a knight splitting his adversary's helm and a lady holding an animal. It is worth noting that this church also possesses, besides these tiles, which are the best of their type in the Chilterns, some of the best wall paintings in Buckinghamshire and the Chilterns.

In Pitstone church are a number of tiles with interesting designs of allegorical devices and even inscriptions. Many small groups exist elsewhere in the Chilterns, generally of similar design: at Aldbury, Chalfont St Giles, Chesham Bois, Edlesborough, Ewelme, Horsenden, Great Mis-

senden, Little Missenden, Monks Risborough, Sarratt and Saunderton.

But the Tring tiles must really claim pride of place on more counts than one. They number ten in all, each about fourteen inches by seven inches, while there are also three fragments. Pictures of most of them hang in Tring church but because of their importance the actual tiles are now in the Victoria and Albert Museum. What is this importance? They are entirely different from all other medieval English tiles and in the following respect.

In the medieval period decorated tiles were made by cutting a stamp or mould and impressing the design on red clay. The depressions were then filled with white clay and the whole dried, glazed and fired. By this method, unlimited numbers of the same design could be produced, and were, as is evident in many churches. The designs covered either one or four tiles, though continuously repeating patterns do appear as well. The Tring tiles, however, were made by the sgraffito technique and are of extreme importance as almost the only existing medieval English examples of this technique applied to anything other than pottery This method involved covering the whole surface of the plain tile with white clay and then scraping it away to reveal the red clay underneath, and so form the design. Such a direct approach demands an artistic competence which would not be found among the makers of the ordinary tiles; the very designs themselves bear this out, for they are of great artistic merit.

These illustrations are negative copies from some of the prints in Tring church

(*a*) A boy falls dead at Christ's feet.

(*b*) Parents complain to Joseph but he is afraid to rebuke Jesus and leaves the task to Mary. Jesus kicks the boy now restored to life.

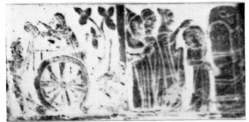

(*a*) Jesus sows corn from his mother's larder and produces a miraculous crop here being harvested.

(*b*) Some parents have locked their children in the oven to keep them away from Jesus who asks what is in the oven; they reply 'pigs'. Jesus opens the door and out run pigs.

(*a*) Jesus before a seated schoolmaster. A boy leans on Jesus' shoulder and drops dead.

(*b*) The parents complain; an uproar is threatened. Joseph rebukes Jesus who restores the boy to life.

(*a*) A boy tried to imitate Jesus sliding down a sunbeam and was killed. The parents remonstrate with Joseph.

(*b*) Jesus restores the boy to life.

(*a*) Jesus in school; the teacher cuffs him when he refuses to speak.

(*b*) Jesus stands before two masters; on the right are two cripples.

(*a*) Jesus was playing with some boys on a hillside when they fell; here he raises them.

(*b*) Jesus had been drawing water with other boys; when he stood his pitcher on a rainbow the other boys tried to imitate him and broke their pitchers. Here Jesus restores them.

Even the subjects are of much interest; most tiles of the time bore abstract patterns, while only a few bore definite illustrations, such as the Chertsey tiles at Little Kimble. The Tring tiles bear individual scenes, two to every rectangular tile, except one, possibly based on the Selden MS now in the Bodleian Library, and representing incidents in the childhood of Christ. These incidents, which appear blasphemous to modern eyes, are now discredited, being taken apparently from the Liber de Infantia, which in turn relied on the Latin Gospel of Thomas. All these stories were popular and well known in medieval times, but are not functional.

The tiles date from the early fourteenth century. From the subject matter it would appear that they are but a few of a set of perhaps sixty, and, to judge from their condition, they may well have been used on the wall rather than on the floor. Otherwise, wall tiles do not seem to have been greatly employed. The tiles were all found within or close to Tring at various times, but it is impossible to determine where they were actually used or whence they came. It is fair supposition that they were *in situ* in Tring church and then thrown out at the time of the Reformation. Because of their quality, however, they probably originated elsewhere, perhaps at the Bonhomme monastery at nearby Ashridge.

The production of tiles continued till the Reformation and then ceased. Many existing tiles were destroyed or, later during the Commonwealth, covered with new flooring slabs. The Victorians, one must suspect, destroyed more than anyone else, and in many instances copied them, stylizing the designs and applying a heavy glaze to create what has been so aptly described as 'lavatory flooring'. Many old tiles, together with memorial slabs and brasses, met a particularly ghastly fate in Turville church where concrete was poured directly on top to raise the floor level to that of the churchyard outside; but this is an extreme case. The Victorians must be credited with restoring many floors to a usable condition from one of potholes and general decay. Even today, many floors are an uneven and motley array of old and new tiles, stone and slate slabs, inscriptions half obliterated, stone with and without brasses, old pitted bricks, marble and wood; some are such 'museums' they are hardly floors at all. Where attention is paid to the problem then it would seem that too great an emphasis is laid on preserving these random pieces to the detriment of a floor's function.

CONCLUSION

It would be very difficult – even dangerous – to draw any far reaching conclusions from such an initial survey as this, particularly with regard to the Chiltern churches as a group. But it would seem that there is not very much evidence to justify the assumption that the churches of the Chiltern Hills in any way form a group; a very great deal of research, including a survey that goes beyond the boundaries of the area, is required to establish this point. Here it should be stated that this chosen grouping is, at least, far less arbitrary than any examination of churches according to counties, as is generally the case.

One point, I think, has been made: that enough material exists in these attractive churches to suggest that they do not deserve the apparent indifference with which they have been treated in the past.

NOTES ON ALL CHURCHES

** indicates points of interest
EE Early English, 1189-1307
DEC Decorated, 1307-1377
PERP Perpendicular, 1377-1485
C century

ALDBURY *St John the Baptist*
Flint-faced walls, stone dressings. Chancel; N chapel;
vestry; nave; N & S aisles; S porch; W tower. No detail
earlier than early 13C. Fabric mainly early 14C, but could
be EE or DEC. N chapel and tall tower, mid-14C.
Extensive restoration 1867.
** Whittingham chapel with fine stone screen, fine tomb
   with effigies; tiles; Verney altar-tomb.
Pleasing interior; good setting. Very attractive village.

AMERSHAM *St Mary*
Flint-faced walls, stone dressings. Chancel; Drake
chapel; Raans chapel; N vestries; S organ chamber; nave;
N & S aisles; N & S transepts; S porch; W tower. Chancel,
nave, transepts, EE. N & S aisles, DEC. Tower, Raans chapel,
S porch, PERP. Drake chapel 18C. Heavy restoration 19C.
** Drake chapel with monuments. Monuments in chancel;
   brasses; modern rood; E window of chancel.
Pleasant town church in fine old town.

BEACONSFIELD *St Mary*
Flint-faced walls, stone dressings. Chancel; N vestry;
S chapel; nave; N & S aisles; N & S porches; W tower.
Entirely rebuilt c1470; largely reconstructed 1869.
** Fine tower; brasses; unusually good 17C chest; fine
   15C recess-tomb; tomb of Edmund Waller in
   churchyard.
Well-restored town church in very fine cross-road position.

BERKHAMSTED *St Peter*
Flint-faced walls, stone dressings. Chancel; S chapel;
central tower; N transept with E aisle; S transept; nave;
N & S aisles; SE chapel. Complex and irregular plan. Nave
unusually long. Oldest parts c1200. Building continued
till 16C. Very bad restoration, early 19C. Extensive but
poor restoration by Butterfield, 1871. Also 1881. Excellent
restoration of interior, 1960.
** 15C tomb with effigies; 2 tomb-chests; brasses; 15C
   screen used as reredos; fine new altar.
Large, handsome town church.

BLEDLOW *Holy Trinity*
Flint-faced walls, clunch dressings. Chancel; nave; N & S
aisles; S porch; W tower. Apparently cruciform before 1200;
rebuilt 13C. Porch 14C. Roof 15C. No drastic
restorations. Restoration 1960-61.
** Windows; modern rood; tower and corbel-table;
   S doorway; Aylesbury font, late 12C; fragmentary
   wall-paintings.
Good village church; fine setting on W scarp of Chilterns.

BRADENHAM *St Botolph*
Flint-faced walls, stone dressings. Chancel; N chapel; nave;
S porch; W tower. Nave c1100; W tower late 15C.
Chancel rebuilt 1863. Restoration 19C.
** Heraldic glass in N chapel; S doorway; modern rood;
   chest; West monument 1648.
Beautiful setting in Wycombe-Risborough valley.

BRITWELL *St Nicholas*
Flint-faced walls, stone dressings. Chancel; nave; S porch.
Rebuilt 19C.
** Norman doorway; brasses.
Remote.

BURNHAM *St Peter*

Flint-faced walls, stone dressing. Chancel; NE vestry, SE tower; nave; N transept; N & S aisles; N & S porches. Fabric 12C; chancel rebuilt early 13C, N transept and N aisle added. S aisle c1250. Extensive 19C restoration. Bell-chamber rebuilt, spire added 1892.
** N transept; brasses; 16C, 17C, 18C monuments. Carved panelling in N transept; altar-rails.
Large village church pleasingly integrated into old village.

CHALFONT ST GILES *St Giles*

Flint-faced walls, stone dressings. Chancel; N vestry; S organ chamber; nave; N & S aisles; S porch; W tower. Begun 12C. Interesting development. Tower demolished 14C; rebuilt 15C. Thorough restoration 1861-3.
** Font c1200; tomb-chest; brasses; texts; exceptional series of 14C wall-paintings in S aisle.
Good village church; very picturesque village.

CHALFONT ST PETER *St Peter*

Brick, stone dressings. Chancel; nave; S chapel; S porch; W tower. Old church collapsed 1708. Rebuilt 1714. 19C, extensively altered, enlarged, Gothicised.
** Brasses.

CHECKENDON *St Peter and St Paul*

Flint-faced walls, stone dressings. Chancel; apse; nave; S porch; W tower. Norman with few alterations. Poor 19C restoration.
** Apse; wall-paintings in apse; brasses; Norman decoration.
Very lovely position.

CHENIES *St Michael*

Flint-faced walls, stone dressings. Chancel; nave; N Bedford chapel; S aisle; S porch; W tower. Entirely rebuilt 15C. Extensive restorations 1861, 1887.
** Aylesbury font late 12C; fabulous monuments to Russell family, Dukes of Bedford, in chapel. *(Special permission)*
Undistinguished church; fine 'model' village.

CHESHAM *St Mary*

Flint-faced walls, stone dressings. Chancel; central tower; N & S transepts; nave; N & S aisles; S porch. Parts 12C; aisles 13C; chancel, tower, mid-14C. Alterations 15C. Considerable restoration by G. G. Scott, 1868-9.
** S porch; modern sedilia; monuments; hatchments.
Over-restored town church. Fine position.

CHESHAM BOIS *St Leonard*

Flint-faced walls, stone dressings. Chancel; vestry; nave; N aisle; SW tower. Only nave and chancel from 14C to 1884. Tower 1887; extensions 1911. Restoration 1951.
** East window of chancel; brasses; tomb-chest, late 16C; 17C pulpit.
Undistinguished church; incongruous in rather remote setting.

CHINNOR *St Andrew*

Flint-faced walls, stone dressings. Chancel; vestry; nave; N & S aisles; N & S porches; W tower. Mainly DEC but some earlier work. Extensively restored 19C.
** Fine series of brasses; early screen c 1350; cross; windows in chancel.
Fine exterior; good position below Chiltern scarp, marred by Chinnor Cement works.

CHOLESBURY *St Leonard*

Flint-faced walls, stone dressings. Chancel; vestry; nave; S porch; W bell-turret. Rebuilt 1872-3.
** S doorway.
Unpretentious, tucked away.

CROWELL

Flint-faced walls, stone dressings. Chancel; nave; S porch; W bell-turret. Norman & DEC. Badly and extensively restored, 19C.
**Transitional font; S doorway.
Very disillusioning.

EATON BRAY *St Mary the Virgin*

Flint-faced walls, stone dressings. Chancel; S chapel; nave; N & S aisles; N & S porches; W tower. Nothing earlier than early 13C when church appears to have been rebuilt and considerably enlarged; church reconstructed around this core in 15C; 19C restoration 1890-1916; vestry 1930.
**Superb arcades, particularly N; beautiful ironwork, 13C, on S door by Thomas of Leighton; fine 13C marble font.
Pleasant small village church below Chiltern scarp.

EDLESBOROUGH *St Mary the Virgin*

Mainly of ashlar limestone. 19C, coated with peeling Roman cement. Chancel; N chancel aisles; nave; N & S aisles; N & S porches; W tower. Parts 13C, 14C. Mainly 15C. Ghastly restoration 1867.

** Corbels in N chapel; tiles; excellent brasses; magnificent
   15C pulpit with soaring spire; fine 15C screen, stalls
   with misericords; tiny gem of 15C stained glass.
Fine church but in poor condition. Excellent position
on mound. Scattered village.

ELLESBOROUGH *St Peter and St Paul*
Flint-faced walls, stone dressings. Chancel; S organ
chamber; vestry; nave; S aisle; S porch; W tower.
Rebuilt 15C; poor and extensive 19C restoration.
** 14C font; monument; Comper reredos.
Pleasing exterior; excellent position on outlying spur of
Chiltern scarp.

EWELME *St Mary the Virgin*
Flint-faced walls, stone dressings. Chancel; vestry;
SE chapel; nave; N & S aisles; N & S porches; W tower.
Entirely rebuilt *c*1440 by Duke of Suffolk; East Anglian
influence. Well restored.
** Beautiful interior; 15C font with soaring spire; angel
   roof in chapel; many brasses; tiles; superb monument
   with effigy and canopy to Alice, Duke of Suffolk, *c*1475.
Lovely church, fine setting.

FAWLEY *St Mary the Virgin*
Flint-faced walls, stone dressings. Chancel; N vestry; nave;
N & S transepts; W tower. Nave 12C; tower late 13C.
Chancel 1748. Restoration 1883, when transepts added.
**Monument; early 18C pulpit and reading desk, and
   other woodwork in chancel, brought from Canons, Little
   Stanmore in Middlessex, in 1747.
Unassuming church; partially isolated.

FINGEST *St Bartholomew*
Rendered flint-rubble walls, stone dressings. Chancel;
nave; S porch; W tower. Nave, tower, early 12C; chancel
13C. 19C restoration.
** Unusually large tower, 24′ square, 60′ high, twin-gabled
   roof; fine west window *c*1230; font.
Bold, striking village church; pleasant village set well
among hills.

FLAUNDEN *St Mary Magdalen*
Flint-rubble walls, stone dressings. Now in ruins. Greek-
cross plan *c*1230. Abandoned 1838; new church some
distance away by Sir Gilbert Scott.
** Font 15C; tiles all over floor of porch. Striking modern
   glass in E window.

FULMER *St James*
Brick walls, stone dressings. Chancel; nave; N porch;
S aisle; W tower. Church rebuilt away from old one, by
Sir Marmaduke Dayrell, 1610. Extensive restoration and
enlarging, 1877, 1884.
**Very fine monument to founder and wife; rare wooden
   Jacobean font; stained glass.
Rather dull exterior; pleasing village.

GREAT GADDESDEN *St John the Baptist*
Flint-rubble walls, plastered; stone dressings. Chancel;
N chapel; nave; N & S aisles; S porch; W tower. Parts
*c*1100; *also* 13C, 14C. Tower 15C. Parts rebuilt 1886.
N chapel 1730. Restoration late 19C.
** Fine S arcade; chests; monuments to Halsey family.
Plain exterior; horrid small village.

LITTLE GADDESDEN *St Peter and St Paul*
Flint-rubble walls, stone dressings. Chancel; N & S chapels;
nave; N & S aisles; S porch; W tower. Largely rebuilt
over the centuries. Parts 15C; rest later. Restorations early
19C and 1880.
** Chest; late 19C pulpit; monuments.
Fine position on open ridge; isolated from 19C model
village.

HAMBLEDEN *St Mary the Virgin*
Flint-faced walls, stone dressings. Chancel; N vestry;
N & S chancel aisles ; N & S transepts; nave; S porch;
W tower. Parts 13C; nave rebuilt 14C; chancel and
S transept enlarged, mid-14C; central tower demolished
1703; W tower 1719-21; restorations and rebuilding 1859
and 1883. Interior decorated 1951, chancel 1953.
** DEC sedilia; brasses; 16C monuments; lovely Cope
   D'Oyley monument; 12C tub font; 15C Nottingham
   alabaster.
Beautiful setting; church stands amid pretty village in one
of loveliest of Chiltern valleys.

GREAT HAMPDEN *St Mary Magdalen*
Flint-faced walls, stone dressings. Chancel; nave; N & S
aisles; S porch; SW tower. Parts mid-14C; tower early
15C; other 15C work. Extensive restoration in 19C.
** S porch; brasses; 17C pulpit; monument to John
   Hampden; 13C font.
Very pleasant interior; lovely, remote setting in grounds of
Hampden house. No village.

LITTLE HAMPDEN

Plastered flint-rubble walls, stone dressings. Chancel; nave; N porch, timber. Mainly 13C; chancel largely rebuilt in 19C. N porch 16C.

** Fragment of 12C stone carving; piscina; picturesque half-timbered porch, unique in Chilterns and Bucks. 18C font; early stone altar-slab; mass of wall-paintings, including perhaps earliest St Christopher.

One of the smallest churches; splendidly situated right among the hills in the tiny hamlet that is Little Hampden.

HEDGERLEY St Mary

Flint-faced walls, stone dressings. Chancel; nave; S porch; W tower. Gothic revival church by Benjamin Ferrey, 1852, close to site of old church.

** 12C font, recarved in 15C; 17C Ten Commandments on canvas with illustrations and explanations, rare.

Fine commanding position on hill in lovely scenery.

HEMEL HEMPSTEAD St Mary

Flint-faced walls, some bricks, Totternhoe stone dressings. Chancel; N & S transepts; NW vestries; central tower; N & S aisles; nave; N & S porches. Complete cruciform church of c1140-1180. Spire, 14C. Some 15C work.

** Norman construction and decoration; vaulted chancel; fine spire, unique in Herts and Chilterns; brasses.

Ghastly restoration inside by Bodley, 1885. Fine dominating church in old town.

HENLEY-ON-THAMES St Mary

Flint-faced walls, some ashlar, stone dressings. Chancel; N & S chapels; nave; double N & S aisles; W tower. Parts are 13C; tower early 16C. Extensive 19C restorations and decorations, not displeasing.

** Monument; Victorian decorations.

Fine church in fine Thames town.

HORSENDEN St Michael and All Angels

Flint-faced walls, ashlar tower, stone dressings. Undivided chancel and nave; W tower. Old nave and tower demolished 1765; new tower built where old nave was. Elaborate restoration 1869.

** 15C screen attached to W wall of nave; tiles.

Delightfully remote setting.

HUGHENDEN St Michael and All Angels

Flint-faced walls, stone dressings. Chancel; N chapel; nave; N aisle; S porch; NW tower. Almost entirely rebuilt 1874-90. N chapel 14C.

** EE font; memorial to Disraeli erected by Queen Victoria; the Hughenden effigies which include 16C forgeries!

Pleasant position within grounds of Hughenden Manor.

IBSTONE St Nicholas

Flint-rubble walls, rendered; stone dressings. Chancel; nave; S porch; W bell-turret. Nave early 12C; chancel 13C; some later work; restoration 1870.

** 12C tub-font; very tall chancel arch, head at apex of soffit; elaborate 15C pulpit; Norman S doorway.

Picturesque tiny church; very remote; beautiful situation overlooking Turville valley.

IPSDEN

Flint-faced walls, stone dressings. Chancel; N chapel; nave; S porch; W bell-cote. Built c1200. Extensive 19C restoration.

** Norman work.

Remote; situated in beautiful countryside.

IVINGHOE St Mary the Virgin

Flint-faced walls, stone dressings. Chancel; central tower; N & S transepts; nave; N & S aisles; N, S & W porches. 12C church rebuilt 13C; largely rebuilt 14C; Much 15C work including clerestory, roofs, W porch. Restorations 1819; c1850; 1871-2.

** Nave roof; brasses; 13C effigy; very elaborate 17C pulpit with tester; 16C lectern; bench-ends.

Very large and unusually fine church for village of this size.

GREAT KIMBLE St Nicholas

Flint-faced walls, stone dressings. Chancel; chancel aisles; nave; N & S aisles; S porch; W tower. Parts 13C; much 14C; clerestory 15C; drastic 19C restorations.

** Magnificent Aylesbury font, late 12C; early chest; 19C screen and chancel decoration.

Pleasing position below scarp.

LITTLE KIMBLE All Saints

Flint-faced walls, stone dressings. Chancel; nave; N & S porches; W bell-cote. Parts 12C; mainly 13C. Extensive 19C restoration.

** 12C tub-font; 17C square pulpit; 6 very fine late 13C Chertsey tiles; very fine wall-paintings, 14C.

Unattractive exterior.

ABBOTS LANGLEY *St Lawrence*
Flint-rubble walls, some ashlar, stone dressings. Chancel;
S chapel; nave; N & S aisles; S porch; W tower. Parts
12C; chancel and S chapel, 14C; aisles rebuilt 15C;
18C S porch; 19C restoration.
** wall-paintings in S chapel; monuments 17C, 18C;
   15C font; 15C roofs.
Pleasant village church.

KINGS LANGLEY *All Saints*
Flint-faced walls, some ashlar, stone dressings. Chancel;
N & S chapels; vestry; nave; N & S aisles; N porch;
W tower. Chancel 13C; parts 14C; extensive rebuilding
15C; W tower and N chapel late 15C; extensive
restoration 1877. Also more recent work.
** Langley tomb late 14C; 15C tomb; very fine 17C pulpit
   with tester; brasses; chest.
Large village church, not particularly attractive.

THE LEE *St John the Baptist*
Rendered flint-rubble walls, stone dressings. Undivided
nave and chancel; S porch; W bell-cote. Early 12C;
some 13C, 14C work. New church built 1868, brick.
Old church used occasionally.
** Piscina and sedile; tub-font 12C; 13C stained glass;
   monuments; texts.
Tiny, very pleasing.

LEWKNOR *St Margaret*
Flint-faced walls, some ashlar, stone dressings. Chancel;
nave; S aisle; N chapel; S porch; W tower. Late Norman;
fine DEC work; 19C restoration.
** Fine 12C font; 16C effigies; superb DEC sedilia;
   monuments.
Plain church; not very attractive in or out.

MARLOW *All Saints*
Chancel; nave; N & S aisles; W tower, lofty spire. 1832.
** Monuments.
Attractive church outside.

MEDMENHAM *St Peter and St Paul*
Flint-faced walls, some ashlar, stone dressings. Chancel;
nave; vestry; N transept; S porch; W tower. Parts Norman;
almost entirely rebuilt 15C; extensive restoration 1839;
restoration 1906; N transept 1925.
** Striking roof; pulpit contains 17C panels; early
   hatchment 1677; 16C stained glass.
Lovely church not far from Thames.

GREAT MISSENDEN
Flint-faced walls; ashlar tower; stone dressings.
Chancel; nave; N & S transepts; N & S aisles; vestry; organ
chamber; N & S porches; W tower. Largely rebuilt 14C;
some 15C work; tower enlarged 16C; poor 19C
restoration; 20C, well-decorated and maintained.
** Niches and blank arcade in chancel; nave arcades;
   15C roof; brasses; Aylesbury font late 12C, bowl recut;
   monuments.
Fine position on hill-side outside village. Fine interior.

LITTLE MISSENDEN *St John the Baptist*
Flint-faced walls, some brick, stone dressings. Chancel;
nave; N chapel; N & S aisles; vestry; S porch; W tower.
Saxon church extensively altered by Normans; some 14C
work; 15C restoration; 18C restoration; 19C restoration;
vestry 1948.
** 12C Aylesbury font; 14C roof; brasses; tiles; chests;
   magnificent wall-paintings, including superb
   St Christopher.
Pleasing village church in backwater.

NORTHCHURCH *St Mary*
Flint-faced walls, ashlar tower, stone dressings. Chancel;
vestry; organ chamber; central tower;
N & S transepts; nave; N aisle; S porch. Parts 13C,
although older church did exist; tower rebuilt 15C; other
15C work; very extensive 19C restoration and building,
aisle, vestry, porch, organ chamber.
** 15C font; superb 15C Flemish chest; stone coffin.
   Attractive church, but dull inside, in busy suburb
   of Berkhampsted.

PENN *Holy Trinity*
Flint-faced walls, some brick, stone dressings. Chancel;
S chapel; nave; S aisle; SW vestry; N & S porches; W
tower. Mainly early 14C; aisle and chapel mid-14C;
15C alterations; 1733, chancel and chapel rebuilt in brick;
1865, E wall of chancel rebuilt in flint; modern
bell-chamber; 19C restoration.
** Lead-font, *c*12C; interesting 16C, 17C brasses;
   hatchments; amazing 15C doom painting on oak boards.
Very pleasant village church, delightful surroundings.

PISHILL
Flint-faced walls, stone dressings; chancel; nave; N porch.
Norman church, rebuilt 19C.
Unattractive.

PITSTONE *St Mary*

Rendered flint-rubble walls, chalk dressings. Chancel; vestry; N chapel; nave; N aisle; S porch; W tower. Parts mid-13C; aisles, late 13C; rebuilding, including N arcade, 15C; 1893 restoration; restoration 1959-60.
** 12C Aylesbury font; 15C roofs; 15C stone reredos; tiles; 17C pulpit with tester; 16C seating; 'Pitstone chest'.
Fine church on chalkfields below scarp, remote.

RADNAGE *St Mary the Virgin*

Flint-rubble walls, partly rendered, stone dressings. Chancel; central tower; nave; N & S porches. Unusual plan. Saxon church did exist. Mainly *c*1120; nave lengthened, 15C, and other work. Chancel reroofed 16C; 19C small restoration.
** Egg-cup font; 17C pulpit; brasses; fine 15C roof; wall-paintings in nave and chancel, best in latter; texts.
Very remote, fine position.

MONKS RISBOROUGH *St Dunstan*

Flint-faced walls, stone dressings. Chancel; organ-chamber; nave; N transept; N & S aisles; S porch; W tower. Largely rebuilt in late 14C and 15C. Tower early 14C. Extensive restoration 1863.
** 12C Aylesbury font; fine 15C work in N transept; bench-ends; 15C screen with weird figures painted on it; fragments of mediaeval glass; tiles; windows.
Pleasantly secluded below scarp.

PRINCES RISBOROUGH *St Mary*

Flint-faced walls, stone dressings. Chancel; organ-chamber; nave; N & S aisles; S porch; W tower. Parts 13C; mainly 14C; some 15C work; drastic restorations 18C. Restorations 1825-30, 1867; new tower and spire begun 1907.
** 13C window, S aisle; 17C pulpit; 14C piscina and sedile.
Attractive town church; not so good inside.

ROTHERFIELD GREYS *St Nicholas*

Flint-faced walls, stone dressings. Chancel; N chapel; nave; N porch; W bell-turret. Some Norman work; mainly EE; extensive 19C restoration.
** Norman font; fine brass; superb Knollys tomb 17C.
Remote, unattractive.

ROTHERFIELD PEPPARD

Flint-faced church, stone dressings. Chancel; nave; N transept; S porch; W bell-turret. Norman; 19C, largely rebuilt.

** Late Norman font; Norman work at E of chancel; fine 18C marquetry reredos.
Pleasant village church.

SARRATT *The Holy Cross*

Flint rubble walls, some bricks and tiles, stone dressings. Chancel; nave; N & S transepts; S porch; W tower. Mainly late 12C; tower 15C; very extensive restoration by Sir Gilbert Scott, 1865, when aisles added.
** Double piscina; monument; 17C pulpit with tester; 12C tomb slab; traces of wall-painting.
Pleasant exterior; dark interior.

SAUNDERTON *St Mary and St Nicholas*

Flint-faced walls, stone dressings. Completely rebuilt, 1888-91. Chancel; nave; S porch; W bell-cote.
** 12C Aylesbury font; modern rood; brass; tiles; piscina.
Unattractive.

ST LEONARD'S *St Leonard*

Plastered walls, stone dressings. Chancel; nave; S porch; W bell-turret. Existed in 12C; rebuilt after Civil War by Lieutenant-General Cornelius Wood. 19C restoration.
** 17C roof; monuments; piscina and sedile.
Delightful secluded church.

STOKENCHURCH *St Peter and St Paul*

Flint-rubble walls, stone dressings. Chancel; nave; N transept; N aisle; S porch; W bell-tower. Parts 12C; 14C, 15C work; 16C N transept; extensive restoration 1847; further building 1893. Restoration 1959.
** Font; brasses; good 14C piscina; monuments.
Unattractive in and out.

STOKE POGES *St Giles*

Flint-faced walls, stone dressings; chapel, brick. Chancel; vestry; Hastings chapel; nave; N tower; N & S aisles; S porch. Parts *c*1100; most rebuilt or added 13C; some 14C, 15C work; chapel 1558; spire demolished 1924; extensive restoration 1897.
** 14C tomb-recess; 13C tomb-slab; the 'Bicycle window'; fine 13C piscina; monuments; brasses; Gray's tomb.
Pleasant village church; poor interior.

SWYNCOMBE *St Botolph*

Flint-faced walls, stone dressings. Chancel; apse; nave; S porch; bell-turret. Saxon church once; Normanised; 19C restoration.

** Norman font; apse with early wall-paintings; pillar.
Very remote; interior spoilt by 20C screen.

TOTTERNHOE *St Giles*
Flint-faced walls, some ashlar, stone dressings. Church
consists of chancel; nave; N & S aisles; S porch; W tower.
Church as it exists today begun in 14C and finally
completed in 16C. 19C restoration.
** Flat 15C nave roof, carved tie-beams; plain 15C font.
Very pleasing village exterior, pinnacled; plain but bright
interior. Below Chiltern scarp; quarries nearby.

TRING *St Peter and St Paul*
Flint-faced walls, some stone, stone dressings. Chancel;
N chapel; vestry; nave; N & S aisles; S porch; W tower.
Almost entirely reconstructed 15C; general repair and
restoration, begun 1861; finally completed 1882, last two
years by Bodley.
** Arcading; enormous monument early 18C; 13C coffin
    slab; the Tring tiles; chests; fine Victorian chancel;
    reredos.
Very fine church in and out; town church pleasantly sited.

TURVILLE *St Mary the Virgin*
Flint-faced walls, clunch dressings. Chancel; vestry;
nave; N aisle; S porch; W tower. 12C, 14C fabric; tower
renovated 17C; beautified 1722; aisle 1733; 19C, church
allowed to decay, vetoed 1875; disastrous restoration;
more satisfactory restoration c1900.
** 12C font; 16C, 18C glass; roof.
Small, cosy church in beautiful village and valley.

WATLINGTON *St Leonard*
Flint-faced walls, ashlar tower, stone dressings. Chancel;
chapel; N & S aisles; nave; W tower; S porch. Some 12C
work; virtually rebuilt 19C; tower 15C.
** Chest; brasses.
Attractive small town church; poor, dark interior.

WENDOVER *St Mary the Virgin*
Flint-faced walls, stone dressings. Chancel; organ-chamber;
vestry; S chapel; nave; N aisle; S aisle; N & S porches;
W tower. Mainly early 14C; parts 13C, 15C; very heavy
19C restorations 1869 by G. E. Street.
** Arcades; brasses.
Pleasant outside; dull inside. Town church.

WOOBURN *St Paul*
Flint-faced walls, stone dressings. Chancel; N chapel;
nave; N & S aisles; W tower. Parts 12C; 14C; tower 15C;
two 19C restorations when much was rebuilt or restored.
** Brasses; chest; Comper screen.
Attractive, large village church.

HIGH WYCOMBE *All Saints*
Flint-faced walls, ashlar tower, stone dressings. Chancel;
N & S chapels; nave; N & S aisles; S porch; W tower.
13C, 14C, work; largely rebuilt 15C. Originally cruciform
church with central tower till 1509-10. G. E. Street
restoration of interior 1873-5; exterior 1887-9.
** S porch; brasses; monuments including vast monument
    to Earl of Shelbourne 1754; large chest; fine 20C reredos.
Very large town church; cramped site; very fine tower.

WEST WYCOMBE *St Lawrence*
Flint-faced walls, stone dressings; some brick dressings.
Chancel; nave; W tower. All early work obscured by 18C
alterations by Sir Francis Dashwood to Classical style.
** Fine 18C interior and fittings; odd 18C font; painting
    of Last Supper by Borgnis; golden ball
    surmounting the tower; open mausoleum.
Fine interior, rather sad state outside; magnificent
position above fine old village.

BIBLIOGRAPHY

The Victoria Counties Histories for
  Buckinghamshire
The Victoria Counties Histories for
  Hertfordshire
The Buildings of England: Buckinghamshire
  by Nikolaus Pevsner. *Penguin*
The Buildings of England: Hertfordshire
  by Nikolaus Pevsner. *Penguin*
The County Books Series: Buckinghamshire
  by Alison Uttley. *Robert Hale*
The County Books Series: Hertfordshire
  by Sir W. Beach Thomas. *Robert Hale*
The County Books Series: Oxfordshire
  by Joanna Cannan. *Robert Hale*
The Companion into Buckinghamshire
  by Maxwell Fraser. *Spurbooks*
The Companion into Hertfordshire
  by W. Branch Johnson. *Methuen*
The Chilterns by J. H. B. Peel. *Paul Elek*

Portrait of the Chilterns by Annan Dickson.
  Robert Hale
Chiltern Country, Face of Britain Series
  by J. Massingham. *Batsford*
A History of Architecture by Banister Fletcher.
  Batsford
Looking for History in British Churches
  by M. D. Anderson. *John Murray*
Parish Churches of England by J. C. Cox.
  Batsford
Portrait of English Churches by Kersting & Vale.
  Batsford
England by Grigson & Smith. *Thames & Hudson*
Liturgy & Architecture by P. Hammond.
  Barrie & Rockliff
English Parish Churches by Hutton & Smith.
  Thames & Hudson
Collins Guide to English Parish Churches
  edited by John Betjeman. *Collins*